SUSE Linux Enterprise Desktop 12 - Subscription Management Tool

A catalogue record for this book is available from the Hong Kong Public Libraries.

Published in Hong Kong by Samurai Media Limited.

Email: info@samuraimedia.org

ISBN 978-988-8406-62-3

Contents

About This Guide

Subscription Management Tool (SMT) for SUSE Linux Enterprise 12 SP1 helps customers to manage their SUSE Linux Enterprise software updates while maintaining corporate firewall policy and regulatory compliance requirements. SMT is a package proxy system that is integrated with the SUSE® Customer Center and provides key SUSE Customer Center capabilities locally at the customer site. It provides a repository and registration target that is synchronized with the SUSE Customer Center, thus maintaining all the capabilities of the SUSE Customer Center while allowing a more secure centralized deployment.

1 Overview

The *Subscription Management Tool Guide* is divided into the following chapters:

SMT Installation

> This chapter introduces the SMT installation process and the SMT Configuration Wizard. You can install the SMT add-on together with your base system during the installation process or on top of an already installed base system. The SMT Configuration Wizard guides you through the individual installation steps.

SMT Server Configuration

> This chapter introduces the YaST configuration module SMT Server. You can set and configure organization credentials, SMT database passwords, and e-mail addresses to send SMT reports, or set the SMT job schedule, and activate or deactivate the SMT service.

Mirroring Repositories on the SMT Server

> This chapter introduces the option to mirror the installation and update sources with YaST.

Managing Repositories with YaST SMT Server Management

> This chapter introduces the option to register client machines on SUSE Customer Center. The client machines must be configured to use SMT.

SMT Reports

> This chapter introduces generated reports based on SMT data. Generated reports contain statistics of all registered machines and products used and of all active, expiring, or missing subscriptions.

SMT Tools and Configuration Files

This chapter introduces the most important scripts, configuration files and certificates shipped with SMT.

Configuring Clients to Use SMT

This chapter introduces the option to configure any client machine to register against SMT and download software updates from there instead of communicating directly with the SUSE Customer Center.

2 Additional Documentation and Resources

Chapters in this manual contain links to additional documentation resources that are available either on the system or on the Internet.

For an overview of the documentation available for your product and the latest documentation updates, refer to http://www.suse.com/documentation.

3 Feedback

Several feedback channels are available:

Bugs and Enhancement Requests

For services and support options available for your product, refer to http://www.suse.com/support/.

To report bugs for a product component, go to https://scc.suse.com/support/requests, log in, and click *Create New*.

User Comments

We want to hear your comments about and suggestions for this manual and the other documentation included with this product. Use the User Comments feature at the bottom of each page in the online documentation or go to http://www.suse.com/doc/feedback.html and enter your comments there.

Mail

For feedback on the documentation of this product, you can also send a mail to doc-team@suse.de. Make sure to include the document title, the product version and the publication date of the documentation. To report errors or suggest enhancements, provide a concise description of the problem and refer to the respective section number and page (or URL).

4 Documentation Conventions

The following typographical conventions are used in this manual:

- /etc/passwd: directory names and file names

- *placeholder*: replace *placeholder* with the actual value

- PATH: the environment variable PATH

- **ls**, --help: commands, options, and parameters

- user: users or groups

- Alt, Alt–F1: a key to press or a key combination; keys are shown in uppercase as on a keyboard

- *File, File › Save As*: menu items, buttons

- *Dancing Penguins* (Chapter *Penguins*, ↑Another Manual): This is a reference to a chapter in another manual.

1 SMT Installation

From version 12 SP1 onwards, SMT is included in SUSE Linux Enterprise Server. To install it, start SUSE Linux Enterprise Server 12 SP1 installation, and click *Software* on the *Installation Settings* screen. Then select the *Subscription Management Tool* pattern on the *Software Selection and System Tasks* screen, and confirm with *OK*.

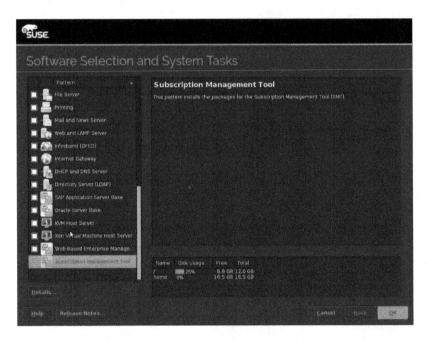

FIGURE 1.1: SMT PATTERN

 Tip: Installing SMT on an Already Installed System

If you already have SUSE Linux Enterprise Server 12 SP1 installed and want to install SMT additionally, follow the same procedure, but instead of including the SMT pattern from the installation screen, simply run *YaST › Software › Software Management*, select *View › Patterns* and select the *SMT* pattern there.

Because SMT depends on other software products, such as MariaDB database engine or Apache Web server, several packages are automatically selected for installation.

It is recommended to check for SMT updates available immediately after installing SUSE Linux Enterprise Server. SUSE continuously releases maintenance updates for SMT, and newer packages are likely to be available compared to those installed from media, for example using the `zypper patch` command.

After the system is installed and updated, do a first-time SMT configuration with *YaST > Network Services > SMT Configuration Wizard*.

1.1 SMT Configuration Wizard

The two-step *SMT Configuration Wizard* helps you configure SMT after SUSE Linux Enterprise Server installation is finished. You can then change the configuration later using the YaST SMT Server Configuration module—see *Chapter 2, SMT Server Configuration*.

1. The *Enable Subscription Management Tool service (SMT)* option is checked by default. Uncheck it only if you want to disable the SMT product.

   If the firewall is enabled, check *Open Port in Firewall* to allow access to the SMT service from remote computers.

   Enter your SUSE Customer Center organization credentials in *User* and *Password*. If you do not know your SUSE Customer Center credentials, refer to *Section 3.1, "Mirroring Credentials"*. Test the entered credentials by pressing the *Test* button. SMT will connect to the Customer Center server using the provided credentials and download some testing data.

   Enter the e-mail address you used for the SUSE Customer Center registration into *SCC E-mail Used for Registration*.

   Your SMT Server URL should contain the URL of the SMT server being configured. It is populated automatically.

   Press *Next* to continue to the second configuration step.

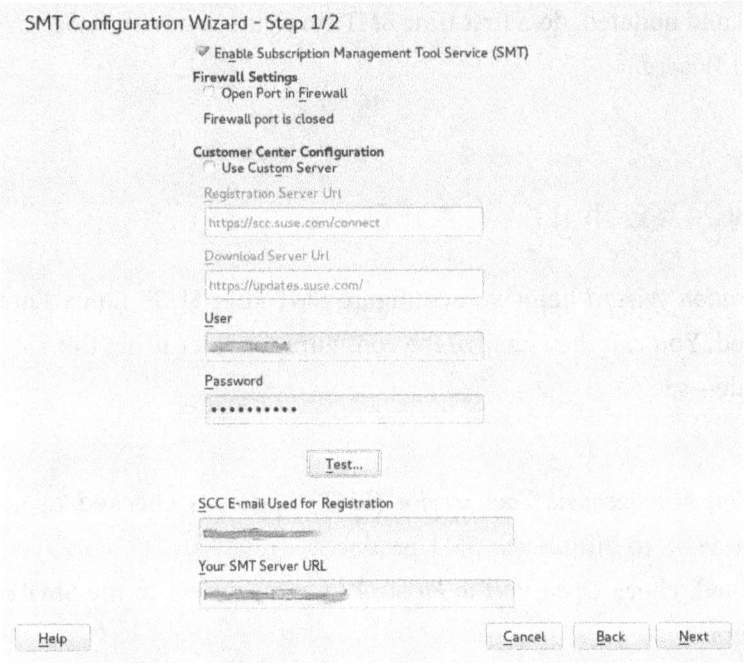

FIGURE 1.2: SMT WIZARD

2. For security reasons, SMT requires a separate user to connect to the database. With the *Database Password for smt User* widget set the database password for that user. Confirm it in the following field.

   Enter all e-mail addresses that SMT should send reports to using the *Add* button. You are also able to *Edit* or *Delete* any incorrect or obsolete addresses.

   Then click *Next*.

3. If the current database root password is empty—as in any freshly installed system—you will be asked to enter it.

4. SMT defaults to communicate with the client hosts via a secure protocol. To use the secured `https` protocol, the SMT server needs to have a server SSL certificate. If it is not created yet, the wizard warns you and offers its creation with *Run CA Management*. Refer to *Book "Security Guide", Chapter 17 "Managing X.509 Certification", Section 17.2 "YaST Modules for CA Management"* for detailed information to manage certificates with YaST.

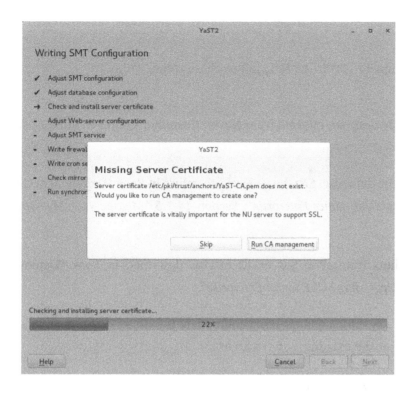

FIGURE 1.3: MISSING SERVER CERTIFICATE

1.2 Upgrading from Previous Versions of SMT

This section contains information about upgrading SMT from previous versions.

Important: Upgrade from Versions Prior to 11 SP3

Direct upgrade path from SMT prior to version 11 SP3 is not supported. You need to upgrade the operating system to SUSE Linux Enterprise Server 11 SP3 or SP4 as described in https://www.suse.com/documentation/sles11/ book_sle_deployment/data/cha_update_sle.html, and at the same time upgrade SMT to version 11 SP3 as described in https://www.suse.com/documentation/smt11/book_yep/data/smt_installation_upgrade.html. Then follow the steps described in *Section 1.2.1, "Upgrade from SMT 11 SP3"*.

1.2.1 Upgrade from SMT 11 SP3

To upgrade SMT from version 11 SP3 to 12 SP1, follow these steps:

1. If you have not already done so, migrate from Novell Customer Center to SUSE Customer Center as described in *Section 1.2.1.1, "Migration to SUSE Customer Center on SMT 11 SP3"*.

2. Back up and migrate the database. See the general procedure in *Book "Deployment Guide", Chapter 14 "Upgrading SUSE Linux Enterprise", Section 14.1.5 "Migrate your MySQL Database"*.

3. Upgrade to SUSE Linux Enterprise Server 12 SP1 as described in *Book "Deployment Guide", Chapter 14 "Upgrading SUSE Linux Enterprise"*.

4. Look if the new `/etc/my.cnf.rpmnew` exists and update it with any custom changes you need. Then copy it over the existing `/etc/my.cnf`:

   ```
   cp /etc/my.cnf.rpmnew /etc/my.cnf
   ```

5. Enable the `smt` target to start at the system boot:

   ```
   systemctl enable smt.target
   ```

   and optionally start it now:

   ```
   systemctl start smt.target
   ```

1.2.1.1 Migration to SUSE Customer Center on SMT 11 SP3

SMT now registers against SUSE Customer Center instead of Novell Customer Center. Therefore you need to switch the registration center on SUSE Linux Enterprise Server 11 before upgrading to SUSE Linux Enterprise Server 12. You can switch to SUSE Customer Center either via a YaST module or command line tools.

Before performing the switch between customer centers, make sure that the target customer center serves all products that are registered against SMT. Both YaST and the command line tools perform a check to find out whether all products can be served with the new registration server.

To perform the migration to SUSE Customer Center via command line, use:

```
smt ncc-scc-migration
```

The migration itself is time-consuming and during the migration process the SMT server may not be able to serve clients that are already registered.

The migration process itself changes the registration server and the proper type of API in the configuration files. No further (configuration) changes are needed on the SMT.

To migrate from Novell Customer Center to SUSE Customer Center via YaST, use the YaST smt-server module.

After migration is done, it is necessary to re-synchronize SMT with the customer center. It is recommended to assure that the repositories are up to date. This can be done using the following commands:

```
smt sync
smt mirror
```

1.3   Enabling SLP Announcements

SMT already includes the SLP service description file (`/etc/slp.reg.d/smt.reg`). To enable SLP announcements of the SMT service, open respective ports in your firewall and enable the SLP service.

```
sysconf_addword /etc/sysconfig/SuSEfirewall2 FW_SERVICES_EXT_TCP "427"
sysconf_addword /etc/sysconfig/SuSEfirewall2 FW_SERVICES_EXT_UDP "427"
insserv slpd
rcslpd start
```

2 SMT Server Configuration

This chapter introduces the YaST configuration module for the SMT server. You can set and configure mirroring credentials, SMT database passwords, and e-mail addresses to send SMT reports to. It also lets you set the SMT job schedule, and activate or deactivate the SMT service.

To configure SMT with SMT Server Configuration, follow these steps:

1. Start the YaST module *SMT Server Configuration* from the YaST control center or by running `yast smt-server` on the command line.

2. To activate SMT, check the *Enable Subscription Management Tool Service (SMT)* option in the *Customer Center Access* tab. If you want to disable SMT, uncheck this option. For more information about activating SMT with YaST, see *Section 2.1, "Activating and Deactivating SMT with YaST"*.

3. If the firewall is enabled, check *Open Port in Firewall*.

4. In the *Customer Center Configuration* section of the *Customer Center Access* tab, you can set the custom server URLs. Set and test credentials for the SUSE Update service. Correct credentials are necessary to enable mirroring from the download server and determine the products that should be mirrored. Also set the e-mail address used for the registration and the URL of your SMT server. For more information, see *Section 2.2, "Setting the Update Server Credentials with YaST"*.

5. In the *Database and Reporting* tab, set the password for the SMT user in the MySQL database and enter the e-mail addresses where reports should be sent. For more information, see *Section 2.3, "Setting SMT Database Password with YaST"* and *Section 2.4, "Setting E-mail Addresses to Receive Reports with YaST"*.

6. In the *Scheduled SMT Jobs* tab, set a schedule of periodic SMT jobs, such as synchronization of updates, SUSE Customer Center registration, and SMT report generation. For more information, see *Section 2.5, "Setting the SMT Job Schedule with YaST"*.

7. If satisfied with the configuration, click *OK*. YaST adjusts the SMT configuration and starts or restarts necessary services.
   If you want to abort the configuration and cancel any changes, click *Cancel*.

Note

When the SMT Configuration applies configuration changes, it checks for the existence of the common server certificate. If the certificate does not exist, you will be asked if the certificate should be created.

2.1 Activating and Deactivating SMT with YaST

YaST provides an easy way to activate or deactivate the SMT service. To activate SMT with YaST, follow these steps:

1. Open the *Customer Center Access* tab of the SMT Configuration.

2. Check the *Enable Subscription Management Tool service (SMT)* option.

    Note

   If not already configured, organization credentials should be configured before activating SMT. For more information about how to set organization credentials with YaST, see *Section 2.2, "Setting the Update Server Credentials with YaST".*

3. Click *Finish* to apply the changes and leave the SMT Configuration.

To deactivate SMT with YaST, follow these steps:

1. Open the *Customer Center Access* tab of the SMT Configuration.

2. Uncheck the *Enable Subscription Management Tool service (SMT)* option.

3. Click *Finish* to apply the changes and leave the SMT Configuration.

When activating SMT, the following important operations are performed by YaST:

- The Apache configuration is changed by creating symbolic links in the `/etc/apache2/conf.d/` directory. Links to the `/etc/smt.d/nu_server.conf` and `/etc/smt.d/smt_mod_perl.conf` files are created there.

- The Apache Web server is started (or reloaded if already running).

- The MariaDB server is started (or reloaded if already running). The smt user and all necessary tables in the database are created as needed.

- The schema of the SMT database is checked. If the database schema is outdated, the SMT database is upgraded to conform to the current schema.

- Cron is adjusted by creating a symbolic link in the `/etc/cron.d/` directory. A link to the `/etc/smt.d/novell.com-smt` file is created there.

When deactivating SMT, the following important operations are performed by YaST:

- Symbolic links created upon SMT activation in the `/etc/apache2/conf.d/` and `/etc/cron.d/` directories are deleted.

- The Cron daemon, the Apache server and the MySQL database daemon are reloaded. Neither Apache nor MySQL are stopped, because they may be used for other purposes than the SMT service.

2.2 Setting the Update Server Credentials with YaST

YaST provides an interface to set and test the download server credentials and the URL of the download server service. To do so, follow these steps:

FIGURE 2.1: SETTING THE UPDATE SERVER CREDENTIALS WITH YAST

1. Open the *Customer Center Access* tab of the SMT Configuration. If the credentials have been already set with YaST or the `/etc/smt.conf` configuration file, they appear in the dialog. Otherwise, the *User* and *Password* fields are blank.

2. If you do not have your credentials, visit SUSE Customer Center to obtain them. For more details, see *Section 3.1, "Mirroring Credentials"*.

3. Enter your user name in *User* and the corresponding password in *Password*.

4. Click *Test* to check the credentials. YaST will try to download a list of available repositories with the provided credentials. If the test succeeds, the last line of the test results will read `Test result: success`. If the test fails, check the provided credentials and try again.

FIGURE 2.2: SUCCESSFUL TEST OF THE UPDATE SERVER CREDENTIALS

5. Enter the *SCC E-mail Used for Registration*. This should be the address you used to register to SUSE Customer Center.
Enter *Your SMT Server URL* if it has not been detected automatically.

6. Click *OK* or continue with other configurations.

2.3 Setting SMT Database Password with YaST

For security reasons, SMT uses its own user in the database. YaST provides an interface for setting up or changing the SMT database password. To set or change the SMT database password with YaST, follow these steps:

1. Open the *Database and Reporting* tab of the SMT Configuration module.

2. Enter the *Database Password for SMT User*. Confirm the password by re-entering it and click *OK*, or continue with other configurations.

2.4 Setting E-mail Addresses to Receive Reports with YaST

YaST SMT provides an interface for setting up a list of e-mail addresses to which SMT reports will be sent. To edit this list of addresses, follow these steps:

1. Open the *Database and Reporting* tab of the SMT Configuration.

2. The list of e-mail addresses is shown in the table. You can *Add*, *Edit*, or *Delete* addresses with the relevant buttons.

3. Click *OK* or continue with other configurations.

The comma-separated list of addresses for SMT reports is written to the `reportEmail` option of the `/etc/smt.conf` configuration file.

2.5 Setting the SMT Job Schedule with YaST

The SMT Configuration module provides an interface to schedule periodic SMT jobs. YaST uses `cron` to schedule configured jobs. If needed, `cron` can be used directly. Five types of periodic jobs can be set:

Synchronization of Updates

Synchronizes with SUSE Customer Center, updates repositories, and downloads new updates.

Generation of Reports

Generates and sends SMT Subscription Reports to addresses defined in *Section 2.4, "Setting E-mail Addresses to Receive Reports with YaST"*.

SCC Registration

Registers all clients to SUSE Customer Center that are not already registered or that changed their data since the last registration.

Job Queue Cleanup

Cleans up queued jobs. It will remove finished or failed jobs from the job queue that are older than 8 days and remove job artifacts that remained in the database as result of an error.

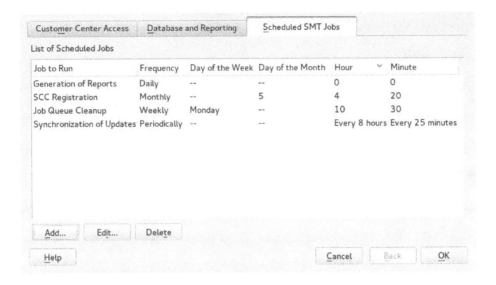

Job to Run	Frequency	Day of the Week	Day of the Month	Hour	Minute
Generation of Reports	Daily	--	--	0	0
SCC Registration	Monthly	--	5	4	20
Job Queue Cleanup	Weekly	Monday	--	10	30
Synchronization of Updates	Periodically	--	--	Every 8 hours	Every 25 minutes

FIGURE 2.3: SMT JOB SCHEDULE CONFIGURATION

To configure the schedule of SMT jobs with YaST, follow these steps:

1. Open the *Scheduled SMT Jobs* tab of the SMT Configuration. The table contains a list of all scheduled jobs, their type, frequency, date, and time to run. You can add, delete or edit these scheduled events.

2. If you want to add a scheduled SMT job, click *Add*. The *Adding New SMT Scheduled Job* dialog opens.
   Choose the synchronization job to schedule. You can choose between *Synchronization of Updates*, *Report Generation*, *SCC Registration*, and *Job Queue Cleanup*.
   Choose the *Frequency* of the new scheduled SMT job. Jobs can be performed *Daily*, *Weekly*, *Monthly*, or *Periodically* (every n-th hour or every m-th minute).
   Set the *Job Start Time* by entering *Hour* and *Minute*. In case of periodic frequency, enter the relevant periods. For weekly and monthly schedules, select *Day of the Week* or *Day of the Month*.
   Click *Add*.

3. If you want to edit a scheduled SMT job (for example, change its frequency, time, or date), select the job in the table and click *Edit*. Then change the desired parameters and click *OK*.

FIGURE 2.4: SETTING SCHEDULED JOB WITH YAST

4. If you want to cancel a scheduled job and delete it from the table, select the job in the table and click *Delete*.

5. Click *OK* to apply the settings and quit the SMT Configuration, or continue with other configurations.

3 Mirroring Repositories on the SMT Server

On the SMT server you can mirror the installation and update repositories locally. This allows you to bypass per-machine downloads and the bandwidth use that goes with it.

> **❗ Important: SUSE Linux Enterprise Server 9 Repositories**
>
> As SUSE Linux Enterprise Server 9 is no longer supported, SMT does not mirror SUSE Linux Enterprise Server 9 repositories.

3.1 Mirroring Credentials

Before you create a local mirror of the repositories, you need appropriate organization credentials. You can get the credentials from SUSE Customer Center.

To get the credentials from SUSE Customer Center, follow these steps:

1. Visit SUSE Customer Center at http://scc.suse.com and log in.

2. If you are member of multiple organizations, chose the organization you want to work with from the drop-down box on the top right.

3. Click *Organization* in the top menu.

4. Click the *Organizational credentials* tab.

5. To show the password, click *Show password*.

The obtained credentials should be set with the YaST SMT Server Configuration module or manually written to the `/etc/smt.conf` file. For more information about the `/etc/smt.conf` file, see *Section 7.2.1, "/etc/smt.conf"*.

Tip: Merging Multiple Organization Site Credentials

SMT can only work with one mirror credential at a time; multiple credentials are not supported. If a customer creates a new company, it results in a new mirror credential. This is not convenient as some products are available via the first set and other products via the second set. To request a merge of credentials, the customer is advised to send an e-mail to Customer_CenterEMEA@novell.com (for EMEA-based customers only—Europe, the Middle East and Africa) with the applicable customer and site IDs. The EMEA PIC team will verify the records. The contact for NALAAP is CustomerResolution@novell.com (North America, Latin America, and Asia Pacific).

3.2 Managing Software Repositories with SMT Command Line Tools

This section describes tools and procedures for viewing information about software repositories available through SMT, configuring these repositories and setting up custom repositories on the command line. For details on the YaST SMT Server Management module, see *Chapter 4, Managing Repositories with YaST SMT Server Management*.

3.2.1 Updating the Local SMT database

The local SMT database needs to be updated periodic with the information downloaded from SUSE Customer Center. These periodical updates can be configured with the SMT Management module, as described in *Section 2.5, "Setting the SMT Job Schedule with YaST"*.

To update the SMT database manually, use the **smt-sync** command. For more information about the **smt-sync** command, see *Section 7.1.2.7, "smt-sync"*.

3.2.2 Enabled Repositories and Repositories That Can Be Mirrored

The database installed with SMT contains information about all software repositories available on SUSE Customer Center. However, the used mirror credentials determine which repositories can really be mirrored. For more information about getting and setting organization credentials, see *Section 3.1, "Mirroring Credentials"*.

Repositories that can be mirrored have the `MIRRORABLE` flag set in the repositories table in the SMT database. The fact that a repository can be mirrored does not mean that it needs to be mirrored. Only repositories with the `DOMIRROR` flag set in the SMT database will be mirrored. For more information about configuring, which repositories should be mirrored, see *Section 3.2.4, "Selecting Repositories to Be Mirrored"*.

3.2.3 Getting Information about Repositories

Use the **smt-repos** command to list available software repositories and additional information. Using this command without any options lists all available repositories, including repositories that cannot be mirrored. In the first column, the enabled repositories (repositories set to be mirrored) are marked with `Yes`. Disabled repositories are marked with `No`. The other columns show ID, type, name, target, and description of the listed repositories. The last columns show whether the repository can be mirrored and staging is enabled.

Use the `--verbose` option, to get additional information about the URL of the repository and the path it will be mirrored to.

The repository listing can be limited to only repositories that can be mirrored or to enabled repositories. To list only repositories that can be mirrored, use the `-m` or `--only-mirrorable` option: **smt-repos -m**.

To list only enabled repositories, use the `-o` or `--only-enabled` option: **smt-repos -o** (see *Example 3.1, "Listing All Enabled Repositories"*).

EXAMPLE 3.1: LISTING ALL ENABLED REPOSITORIES

```
tux:~ # smt-repos -o

.--------------------------------------------------------------------------.
| Mirr| ID | Type | Name          | Target   | Description          | Can be M| Stag|
+-----+----+------+---------------+----------+----------------------+---------+-----+
```

```
| Yes |  1 | zypp | ATI-Driver-SLE11-SP2     | --             | ATI-Driver-SLE11-SP2                | Yes  | Yes |
| Yes |  2 | zypp | nVidia-Driver-SLE11-SP2  | --             | nVidia-Driver-SLE11-SP2             | Yes  | No  |
| Yes |  3 | nu   | SLED11-SP2-Updates       | sle-11-x86_64  | SLED11-SP2-Updates for sle-11-x86_64 | Yes | No  |
| Yes |  4 | nu   | SLES11-SP1-Updates       | sle-11-x86_64  | SLES11-SP1-Updates for sle-11-x86_64 | Yes | Yes |
| Yes |  5 | nu   | SLES11-SP2-Core          | sle-11-x86_64  | SLES11-SP2-Core for sle-11-x86_64   | Yes  | No  |
| Yes |  6 | nu   | SLES11-SP2-Updates       | sle-11-i586    | SLES11-SP2-Updates for sle-11-i586  | Yes  | No  |
| Yes |  7 | nu   | WebYaST-Testing-Updates  | sle-11-i586    | WebYaST-Testing-Updates for sle-11-i586 | Yes | No  |
'-----+----+------+--------------------------+----------------+-------------------------------------+------+-----'
```

You can also list only repositories with a particular name or show information about a repository with a particular name and target. To list repositories with a particular name, use the **smt-repos** *repository_name* command. To show information about a repository with a particular name and target, use the **smt-repos** *repository_name target* command.

To get a list of installation repositories from remote, see *Section 8.7, "Listing Accessible Repositories"*.

3.2.4   Selecting Repositories to Be Mirrored

Only enabled repositories can be mirrored. In the database, the enabled repositories have the DOMIRROR flag set. Repositories can be enabled or disabled using the **smt-repos** command.

To enable one or more repositories, follow these steps:

1. If you want to enable all repositories that can be mirrored or just choose one repository from the list of all repositories, run the **smt-repos -e** command.

   You can limit the list of repositories by using the relevant options. To limit the list to only repositories that can be mirrored, use the -m option: **smt-repos -m -e**. To limit the list to only repositories with a particular name, use the **smt-repos -e** *repository_name* command. To list only a repository with a particular name and target, use the command **smt-repos -e** *repository_name target*.

   If you want to enable all repositories belonging to a certain product, use the --enable-by-prod or -p option followed by the name of the product and, optionally, its version, architecture, and release:

   ```
   smt-repos -p product[,version[,architecture[,release]]]
   ```

For example, to enable all repositories belonging to SUSE Linux Enterprise Server 10 SP3 for PowerPC architecture, use the **smt-repos -p SUSE-Linux-Enterprise-Server-SP3,10,ppc** command. The list of known products can be obtained with the **smt-list-products** command.

2. If more than one repository is listed, choose the one you want to enable by specifying its ID listed in the repository table and pressing Enter . If you want to enable all the listed repositories, use a and press Enter .

To disable one or more repositories, follow these steps:

1. If you want to disable all enabled repositories or just choose one repository from the list of all repositories, run the **smt-repos -d** command.
   If you want to choose the repository to be disabled from a shorter list, or if you want to disable all repositories from a limited group, you can use any of the available options to limit the list of repositories. To limit the list to only enabled repositories, use the -o option: **smt-repos -o -d**. To limit the list to only repositories with a particular name, use the **smt-repos -d** *repository_name* command. To list only a repository with a particular name and target, use the **smt-repos -d** *repository_name target* command.

2. If more than one repository is listed, choose which one you want to disable by specifying its ID listed in the repository table shown and pressing Enter . If you want to disable all the listed repositories, use a and press Enter .

3.2.5 Deleting Mirrored Repositories

You can delete mirrored repositories that are no longer used. If you delete a repository, it will be physically removed from the SMT storage area.

To delete a repository with a particular name, use the **smt-repos --delete** command. To delete the repository in a namespace, specify the --namespace *dirname* option.

--delete lists all repositories, and by entering the ID number or by entering the name and target you can delete the specified repositories. If you want to delete all repositories, enter *a*.

Note: Detecting Repository IDs

Every repository has a sha1sum that you can use as an ID. You can get the repository's sha1sum by calling `smt-repos -v`.

3.2.6 Mirroring Custom Repositories

Using SMT you can also mirror repositories that are not available at the SUSE Customer Center. Those repositories are called "custom repositories". Use the `smt-setup-custom-repos` command for this purpose. Custom repositories can also be deleted.

When adding a new custom repository, `smt-setup-custom-repos` adds a new record in the database, and sets the *mirror* flag to *true* by default. If needed, you can disable mirroring later.

To set up a custom repository to be available through SMT, follow these steps:

1. If you do not know the ID of the product the new repositories should belong to, use `smt-list-products` to get the ID. For the description of the `smt-list-products`, see *Section 7.1.2.4, "smt-list-products"*.

2. Run

   ```
   smt-setup-custom-repos --productid product_id \
   --name repository_name --exturl repository_url
   ```

   In this command *product_id* is the ID of the product the repository belongs to, *repository_name* represents the name of the repository and *repository_url* is the URL the repository is available at. In case the added repository needs to be available for more than one product, specify the IDs of all products that should use the added repository.

   For example, to set My repository available at http://example.com/My_repository to the products with the IDs 423, 424, and 425, use the following command:

   ```
   smt-setup-custom-repositories --productid 423 --productid 424 \
   --productid 425 --name 'My_repository' \
   --exturl 'http://example.com/My_repository'
   ```

Note: Mirroring Unsigned Repositories

In its default configuration, SUSE Linux Enterprise 10 does not allow the use of unsigned repositories. Therefore, if you want to mirror unsigned repositories and use them on client machines, be aware that the package installation tool—YaST or **zypper**—will ask you whether to use repositories that are not signed.

To remove an already-set custom repository from the SMT database, use **smt-setup-custom-repositories --delete** *ID*, where *ID* represents the ID of the repository to be removed.

3.3 The /srv/www/htdocs Structure for SLE 11

The path to the directory containing the mirror is set by the `MirrorTo` option in the `/etc/smt.conf` configuration file. For more information about `/etc/smt.conf`, see *Section 7.2.1, "/etc/smt.conf"*. If the `MirrorTo` option is not set to the Apache htdocs directory `/srv/www/htdocs/`, the following links need to be created. In case the directories already exist, they need to be removed prior to creating the link (the data from those directories will be lost!):

* `/srv/www/htdocs/repo/$RCE` should point to `/MirrorTo/repo/$RCE/`

* `/srv/www/htdocs/repo/RPMMD` to `/MirrorTo/repo/RPMMD/`

* `/srv/www/htdocs/repo/testing` to `/MirrorTo/repo/testing/` and

* `/srv/www/htdocs/repo/full` to `/MirrorTo/repo/full/`

The directory specified by the option `MirrorTo` and the subdirectories listed above must exist. Files, directories and links in `/MirrorTo` need to belong to the user `smt` and the group `www`.

For example, if the `MirrorTo` is set to `/mirror/data`:

```
l /srv/www/htdocs/repo/
total 16
lrwxrwxrwx 1 smt   www     22 Feb  9 14:23 $RCE -> /mirror/data/repo/$RCE/
drwxr-xr-x 4 smt   www   4096 Feb  9 14:23 ./
drwxr-xr-x 4 root  root  4096 Feb  8 15:44 ../
lrwxrwxrwx 1 smt   www     23 Feb  9 14:23 RPMMD -> /mirror/data/repo/RPMMD/
lrwxrwxrwx 1 smt   www     22 Feb  9 14:23 full -> /mirror/data/repo/full/
```

```
drwxr-xr-x 2 smt  www  4096 Feb  8 11:12 keys/
lrwxrwxrwx 1 smt  www    25 Feb  9 14:23 testing -> /mirror/data/repo/testing/
drwxr-xr-x 2 smt  www  4096 Feb  8 14:14 tools/
```

The links can be created using the **ln -s** commands. For example:

```
for LINK in \$RCE RPMMD full testing; do
ln -s /mirror/data/repo/${LINK}/ && chown -h smt.www ${LINK}
done
```

 Note: The /srv/www/htdocs/repo **Directory**

The /srv/www/htdocs/repo directory must not be a symbolic link.

3.4 The /srv/www/htdocs Structure for SLE 12

The repository structure in the /srv/www/htdocs directory matches the structure as it comes from SUSE Customer Center. There are the following directories in the structure (selected examples, similar for other products and architectures):

```
repo/SUSE/Products/SLE-SDK/12/x86_64/product/
```

contains the -POOL repository of SDK (the GA version of all packages):

```
repo/SUSE/Products/SLE-SDK/12/x86_64/product.license/
```

contains EULA associated with the product:

```
repo/SUSE/Updates/SLE-SDK/12/x86_64/update/
repo/SUSE/Updates/SLE-SDK/12/s390x/update/
repo/SUSE/Updates/SLE-SERVER/12/x86_64/update/
```

contain update repositories for respective products:

```
repo/full/SUSE/Updates/SLE-SERVER/12/x86_64/update/
repo/testing/SUSE/Updates/SLE-SERVER/12/x86_64/update/
```

contain repositories optionally created for staging of respective repositories.

3.5 Using the Test Environment

You can mirror repositories to a test environment instead of the production environment. The test environment can be used with a limited number of client machines before the tested repositories are moved to the production environment. The test environment can be run on the main SMT server.

The testing environment uses the same structure as the production environment, but it is located in the `/srv/www/htdocs/repos/testing/` subdirectory.

To mirror a repository to the testing environment, you can use the *Staging* tab in the YaST SMT Management module, or the command **smt-staging**.

To register a client in the testing environment, modify `/etc/SUSEConnect` on the client machine by setting:

```
namespace: testing
```

To move the testing environment to the production environment, manually copy or move it using the **cp -a** or **mv** command.

You can enable "staging" for a repository in the *Repositories* tab of the SMT Management module or with the **smt-repos** command. The mirroring happens automatically to `repo/full/`.

If you have an SLE11-based Update repository with patches, SMT tools can help you with the management. With these tools you can select patches and create a snapshot and copy it into `repo/testing/`. After tests are finished you can copy the contents of `repo/testing` into the production area `/repo`.

SLE10-based Update repositories are not supported by SMT tools. Not all of these repositories support selective staging. In this case you must mirror the complete package.

Recommended work flow:

```
repo => repo/full,
repo/full => repo/testing,
repo/testing => repo
```

3.6 Testing and Filtering Update Repositories with Staging

You can test repositories on any clients with **smt-staging** before moving them to the production environment. You can select new update repositories manually to be installed on clients.

For staging, you can either use the **smt-staging** command, or use the YaST SMT Management module. For more details, see *Section 4.3, "Staging Repositories"*.

Repositories with staging enabled are mirrored to the */MirrorTo/*repo/full subdirectory. This subdirectory is usually not used by your clients. Incoming new updates are not automatically visible to the clients before you get a chance to test them. Later you can generate a testing environment of this repository, which goes to */MirrorTo/*repo directory.

If you have an SLE 11-based update repository with patches, SMT tools can help you with the management. With these tools you can select patches and create a snapshot and put it into repo/testing/. After tests are finished you can put the content of repo/testing into the production area /repo. repo/testing/ and /repo is called the "default" staging group. You can create additional staging groups as needed with the **smt-staging creategroup** command.

 ## Note: SLE 10-based Update Repositories

SLE 10-based Update repositories are not supported by SMT tools. Not all of these repositories support selective staging. In this case you need to mirror the complete package.

Enabling Staging

To enable or disable staging, use the **smt-repos** command with --enable-staging or -s:

```
smt-repos --enable-staging
```

You can enable the required repositories by entering the ID number or by entering the name and target. If you want to enable all repositories enter *a*.

Generating Testing and Production Snapshots

To create the testing repository in the "default" staging group enter:

```
smt-staging createrepo Repository_ID --testing
```

Now you can test the installation and functionality of the patches in testing clients. If no problems are discovered during testing, create the production repository by entering:

```
smt-staging createrepo Repository_ID --production
```

To create testing and production repositories in a named staging group first create the group and then the repositories in this group:

```
smt-staging creategroup Groupname Testingdir Productiondir
smt-staging createrepo --group Groupname Repository_ID --testing
smt-staging createrepo --group Groupname Repository_ID --production
```

This can help you if you, for example, want to combine SLES11-SP1-Updates and SLES11-SP2-Updates of the sle-11-x86_64 architecture into one repository of a group:

```
smt-staging creategroup SLES11SP1-SP2-Up test-sp1-sp2 prod-sp1-sp2
smt-staging createrepo --group SLES11SP1-SP2-Up \
  SLES11-SP1-Updates sle-11-x86_64 --testing
smt-staging createrepo --group SLES11SP1-SP2-Up \
  SLES11-SP2-Updates sle-11-x86_64 --testing
smt-staging createrepo --group SLES11SP1-SP2-Up \
  SLES11-SP1-Updates sle-11-x86_64 --production
smt-staging createrepo --group SLES11SP1-SP2-Up \
  SLES11-SP2-Updates sle-11-x86_64 --production
```

For group names, these characters are allowed: -_, a-zA-Z, and 0-9.

Filtering Patches

You can allow or forbid all or selected patches with the **allow** or **forbid** commands by their ID or Category:

```
smt-staging forbid --patch ID
smt-staging forbid --category Categoryname
```

Signing Changed Repositories

If you filter one or more patches from a repository, the original signature becomes invalid. The repository needs to be signed again. The **smt-staging createrepo** command takes care of that automatically if you configure the SMT server.

To enable signing of changed metadata, the admin needs to generate a new signing key. This can be done with GPG like this:

```
mkdir some_dir
gpg --gen-key --homedir some_dir
sudo mv some_dir /var/lib/smt/.gnupg
sudo chown smt:users -R /var/lib/smt/.gnupg
sudo chmod go-rwx -R /var/lib/smt/.gnupg
```

Then the ID of the newly generated key, as seen in the **gpg --gen-key** command output, must be written into `/etc/smt.conf`, option `signingKeyID`.

At this point the clients do not know about this new key. To import the new key to clients during their registration, the following can be done:

```
sudo -u smt gpg --homedir /var/lib/smt/.gnupg \
  --export -a signingKeyID \
  > /MirrorTo/repo/keys/smt-signing-key.key
```

In this example, `MirrorTo` stands for the base directory where repositories will be mirrored. Once done, clients can import this key during the registration process.

Registering Clients in the Testing Environment

To register a client in the testing environment, modify the `/etc/SUSEConnect` on the client machine by setting:

```
namespace: testing
```

4 Managing Repositories with YaST SMT Server Management

You can use the YaST SMT Server Management module for day-to-day management. SMT Server Management enables and disables the mirroring of repositories, the staging flag for repositories, and performs the mirroring and staging.

4.1 Starting SMT Management Module

SMT Management is a YaST module. To start the module, do one of the following:

- Start YaST and select *Network Services*, then *SMT Server Management*.

- Enter **yast2 smt** in the command line as <u>root</u>.

The SMT Management application window opens with the *Repositories* tab active.

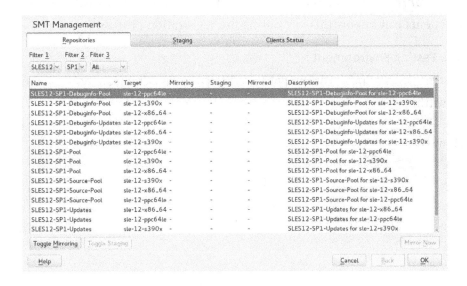

FIGURE 4.1: LIST OF REPOSITORIES

4.2 Viewing and Managing Repositories

In the *Repositories* tab, you can see the list of all available package repositories for SMT. For each repository, the list shows the repository's name, target product and architecture, mirroring and staging flag, date of last mirroring, and a short description. You can sort the list by clicking the relevant column's header, and scroll the list items using the scrollbars on the window's right side.

4.2.1 Filtering Repositories

You can also filter out groups of repositories with the *Filter* drop-down box in the upper left part of the window. The filter list items are collected and assembled dynamically from the first word of the repositories' names. If you use a filter to limit the number of displayed repositories, you can always go back and view all of them by selecting *All* from the *Filter* drop-down box. You can also use more than one filter in sequence.

4.2.2 Mirroring Repositories

Before you can start to offer package repositories, you need to create a local mirror of their packages. To do so, follow this procedure:

1. From the list, select the line containing the name of the repository you want to mirror.

2. Click the selected line to highlight it.

3. Click the *Toggle Mirroring* button in the lower left part of the window. In the *Mirroring* column of the selected repository, a check mark appears. If the repository was already selected for mirroring before, the check mark will disappear, and the repository will not be mirrored anymore.

4. Hit the *Mirror Now* button and the repository will be mirrored immediately.

5. A pop-up window appears with the information about mirroring status and result.

6. Click OK and the original window with the list of repositories will be refreshed.

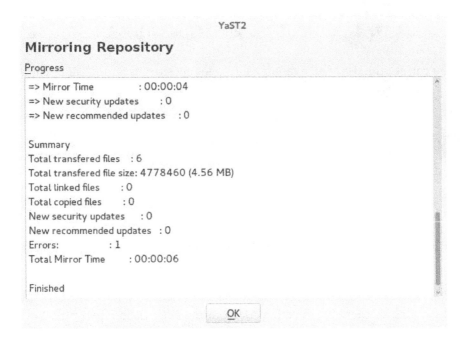

FIGURE 4.2: STATUS OF MIRRORING PROCESS

4.3 Staging Repositories

After the mirroring is finished, you can stage the mirrored repositories. In SMT, *staging* is a process where you create either testing or production repositories based on the mirrored ones. The testing repository helps you examine the repository and its packages before you make them available in a production environment. To make repositories available for staging, do the following:

1. From the repository list, select the line containing the name of the repository you want to manage.

2. Click the selected line, highlighting it.

3. Click the *Toggle Staging* button in the lower left part of the window next to the *Toggle Mirroring* button. In the *Staging* column of the selected repository, a check mark appears. If the repository was already selected for staging before, the check mark will disappear, and the repository will not be available for staging.

4. Repeat steps 1 to 3 for all directories whose staging flag you wish to change.

Staging Repositories

Important: Toggle Staging Button Not Active

You can only stage the repositories that were previously selected for mirroring. If it is not the case, the *Toggle Staging* button will not be active.

Once you mirror the repositories and make them available for staging, click the *Staging* tab. In the upper left part of the window, there is a *Repository Name* drop-down box of all repositories which are available for staging. There the repository names have the name of the staging group attached in parentheses. Select the one you want to stage and a list of packages of this repository appears below. Information about the patch name, its version and category, testing and production flags, and a short summary is available for each patch.

Next to the *Repository Name* drop-down box, there is a *Patch Category* filter. It helps you to list only the patches that belong to one of the predefined categories.

If the selected repository allows for patch filtering, you can toggle the status flag for individual patches. Do so by clicking the *Toggle Patch Status* button in the lower left part of the window.

Before creating a repository of packages that are available in the *production* environment, you need to create and test the *testing* repository. Click the *Create Snapshot* drop-down box and select the *From Full Mirror to Testing* menu item. A small pop-up window appears informing you about the staging process. After the testing repository snapshot is created, the relevant check marks in the *Testing* column will be displayed.

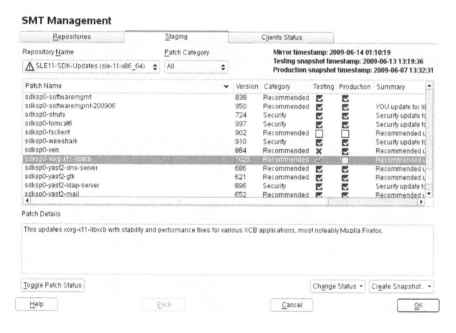

FIGURE 4.3: TESTING SNAPSHOT CREATED

! Important: Creating a Production Snapshot

After you enable *staging* for an update repository, you need to create its *production* snapshot to make it available to the clients. Otherwise the clients will not be able to find the update repository.

After you have examined the newly created testing repository, you can safely create a production one. Click the *Create Snapshot* drop-down box and select the *From Testing to Production* menu item. A small pop-up window appears informing you about linking the testing repository to the production one. After the production snapshot is created, the relevant check marks in the *Production* column will be displayed. Also, a green check mark appears in the *Repository Name* drop-down box.

4.4   Checking the Client Status

The third tab called *Clients Status* contains the status information about all the clients that use the repositories on your SMT server. It is divided into two main parts: the list of the clients and the detailed information.

You can read the client's host name, the date and time of the last network contact with the SMT server, and its update status. The update status can be one of the following:

Up-to-date

The client packages are updated to their last version available in the production repository.

Updates available

This status means that there are updates available for the client that are either `optional` or `recommended`.

Critical

Either `security` patches or `package manager` patches are available for the client.

In the lower part of the window, more detailed information about the selected client is available. It usually consists of extended status information and detailed information about the number and types of available updates.

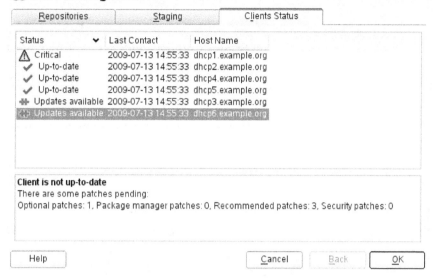

FIGURE 4.4: CLIENTS STATUS

5 Managing Client Machines with SMT

SMT lets you register and manage client machines on SUSE Customer Center. Client machines must be configured to use SMT. For information about configuring clients to use SMT, see *Chapter 8, Configuring Clients to Use SMT*.

5.1 Listing Registered Clients

To list SMT-registered client machines, use the **smt-list-registrations** command. The following information is listed for each client: its *Unique ID*, *Hostname*, date and time of *Last Contact* with the SMT server, and the Software *Product* the client uses.

5.2 Deleting Registrations

To delete a registration from SMT and SUSE Customer Center, use the following command. To delete multiple registrations, the option -g can be used several times.

```
smt-delete-registration -g Client_ID
```

The ID of the client machine to be deleted can be determined from the output of the **smt-list-registrations** command.

5.3 Manual Registration of Clients at SUSE Customer Center

The **smt-register** command registers clients at SUSE Customer Center. All clients that are currently not registered or whose data has changed since the last registration are registered.

To register clients whose registration has failed, use the --reseterror option. This option resets the SCC registration error flag and tries to submit failed registrations again.

5.4 Scheduling Periodic Registrations of Clients at SUSE Customer Center

SMT module allows for the easy scheduling of client registrations. In the default configuration, registrations are scheduled to repeat every 15 minutes. To create or modify a new registration schedule, follow these steps:

1. Start YaST *SMT Configuration* module (`yast2 smt-server`).

2. Go to the *Scheduled SMT Job*.

3. Select any *SCC Registration* job and click *Edit* if you want to change its schedule.
   To create a new registration schedule, click *Add* and select *SCC Registration* as *Job to Run*.

4. Choose the *Frequency* of the scheduled SMT job. You can perform jobs *Daily*, *Weekly*, *Monthly*, or *Periodically* (every n-th hour or every m-th minute).
   Set the *Job Start Time* by entering the *Hour* and *Minute* or, in case of periodic frequency, the relevant periods. For weekly and monthly schedules, select the *Day of the Week* or the *Day of the Month* the mirroring should occur.

    Note: Lowest Registration Frequency

   Do not set the frequency lower than 10 minutes, because the maximum value of the `rndRegister` is 450 (7.5 minutes). If the frequency is lower, it may occur that the started process is still sleeping when the next process starts. In this case, the second request will exit.

5. Click either *OK* or *Add* and *Finish*.

Scheduling of SMT jobs in general is covered in *Section 2.5, "Setting the SMT Job Schedule with YaST"*.

YaST uses `cron` to schedule SUSE Customer Center registrations and other SMT jobs. If you do not want to use YaST, use `cron` directly.

To disable automatic registration, change the `forwardRegistration` value in the `[LOCAL]` section of the `/etc/smt.conf` configuration file to `false`.

6 SMT Reports

This chapter introduces reports generated based on the SMT and SUSE Customer Center data. The reports generated contain statistics of all the registered machines, products used and all active, expiring or missing subscriptions.

 Note: Assignment of Reports

If you are using more than one SMT server in your environment, generated reports may not represent all of the SMT servers or machines in your environment. For the complete statistics of all your registered machines, refer to the information in the SUSE Customer Center.

6.1 Report Schedule and Recipients

Generated SMT reports can be sent to a defined list of e-mail addresses periodically. To create or edit this list, and to set the frequency of the reports, use the YaST SMT Configuration module. How to configure this list is described in *Section 2.4, "Setting E-mail Addresses to Receive Reports with YaST"*. Configuration of the report schedule is described in *Section 2.5, "Setting the SMT Job Schedule with YaST"*.

The list can also be edited manually in the `reportEmail` option of the `/etc/smt.conf` configuration file. For more information about editing the list of addresses directly, see *Section 7.2.1.6, "[REPORT] Section of /etc/smt.conf"*. To set the frequency of reports manually, you can directly edit the `smt-gen-report` lines of the crontab in `/etc/cron.d/novell.com-smt`. For more information about the crontab format, see **man 5 crontab**.

Reports, including those created as a scheduled SMT job, are created by the **smt-report** command. This command has various parameters. To edit parameters used with scheduled commands, edit the `/etc/smt.d/smt-cron.conf` configuration file. For more information, see *Section 7.2.2, "/etc/smt.d/smt-cron.conf"*.

6.2 Report Output Formats and Targets

SMT reports can be printed to the standard output, exported to one or multiple files (in CSV format) and be mailed to the defined list of e-mail addresses. Use the following options for the **smt-report** command:

--quiet or -q

>   Suppress output to STDOUT and run **smt-report** in quiet mode.

--file or -F

>   Export report to one or several files. By default, the report will be written to a single file, rendered as tables. Optionally, the file name or whole path may be specified after the parameter: `--file filename`. If no file name is specified, a default file name containing a time stamp is used. However, SMT will not check if the file or files already exist.
>
>   In CSV (Comma-Separated Value) mode the report will be written to multiple files, therefore the specified file name will expand to `[path/]filename-reportname.extension` for every report.

--csv or -c

>   The report will be exported to multiple files in CSV format. The first line of each *.csv file consists of the column names, then the data starts on line two. It is recommended to use the `--csv` parameter together with the `--file` parameter. If the specified file name contains a `.csv` extension, the report format will be CSV (as if the `--csv` parameter was used).

--mail or -m

>   Activate mailing of the report to the addresses configured with the YaST SMT Configuration module and written in `/etc/smt.conf`. The report will be rendered as tables.

--attach or -a

>   Attach the report to the mails in CSV format. This option should only be used together with the `--mail` option.

--pdf

>   The report will be exported to multiple files in pdf format.

--xml

>   The report will be exported to multiple files in xml format.

Note: Disabling Sending Attachments

If you want to disable sending CSV attachments with report mails, edit the `/etc/smt.d/smt-cron.conf` configuration file as follows: remove the `--attach` option from the `REPORT_PARAMS` value. The default line reads: `REPORT_PARAMS="--mail --attach -L /var/log/smt-report.log"`. To disable CSV attachments, change it to: `REPORT_PARAMS="--mail -L /var/log/smt-report.log"`.

If you have disabled CSV attachments but need them occasionally, you can send them manually with the **smt-report --mail --attach -L /var/log/smt-report.log** command.

7 SMT Tools and Configuration Files

This chapter describes the most important scripts, configuration files and certificates shipped with SMT.

7.1 Important Scripts and Tools

There are two important groups of SMT commands: The `smt` command with its sub-commands is used for managing the mirroring of updates, registration of clients, and reporting. The `systemd` `smt.target` is used for starting, stopping, restarting the SMT service and services that SMT depends on, and for checking their status.

7.1.1 SMT JobQueue

Since SUSE Linux Enterprise version 11, there is a new SMT service called SMT JobQueue. It is a system to delegate *jobs* to the registered clients.

To enable JobQueue, the `smt-client` package needs to be installed on the SMT client. The client then pulls jobs from the server via a cron job (every 3 hours by default). The list of jobs is maintained on the server. Jobs are not pushed directly to the clients and processed immediately, but the client asks for them. Therefore, a delay of several hours may occur.

Every job can have its parent job, which sets a dependency. The child job only runs after the parent job successfully finished. Job timing is also possible: a job can have a start time and an expiration time to define its earliest execution time or the time the job will expire. A job may also be persistent. It is run repeatedly with a delay. For example, a patch status job is a persistent job that runs once a day. For each client, a patch status job is automatically generated after it registers successfully against an SMT 11 server. The patchstatus information can be queried with the **smt-client** command. For already registered clients, you can add patchstatus jobs manually with the **smt-job** command.

You can manipulate, list, create or delete the jobs. For this reason, the command line tool **smt-job** was introduced. For more details on **smt-job**, see *Section 7.1.2.3, "smt-job"*.

Note: Overriding the Automatic Creation of Patch Status Jobs

When creating a software push or an update job, normally a non-persistent patch status job will be added automatically with the parent id set to the id of the new job. To disable this behavior, use the `--no-autopatchstatus` option.

SMT is not intended to be a system to directly access the clients or to immediately report the results back; it is a longtime maintenance and monitoring system rather than a live interaction tool.

 Note: Job Time Lag Limitation

The client will process one job at a time, report back the result, and then ask for the next job. If you create a persistent job with a time lag of only a few seconds, it will be repeated forever and block other jobs of this client. Therefore, adding jobs with a time lag smaller than one minute is not supported.

7.1.2   /usr/sbin/smt Commands

The main command to manage the SMT is **smt** (`/usr/sbin/smt`). The **smt** command should be used together with various sub-commands described in this section. If the **smt** command is used alone, it prints a list of all available sub-commands. To get help for individual sub-commands, use **smt** *subcommand* --help.

The following sub-commands are available:

- `smt-client`

- `smt-delete-registration`

- `smt-job`

- `smt-list-products`

- `smt-list-registrations`

- `smt-mirror`

- `smt-scc-sync`

- `smt-register`

- `smt-report`

- `smt-repos`

- `smt-setup-custom-catalogs`

- `smt-setup-custom-repos`

- `smt-staging`

- `smt-support`

- `smt-sync`

There are two syntax types you can use with the `smt` command: either use `smt` followed by a sub-command or use a single command (composed of `smt`, dash, and the sub-command of your choice). For example, it is possible to use either `smt mirror` or `smt-mirror`, as both have the same meaning.

 Note: Conflicting Commands

Depending on your `$PATH` environment variable, the SMT `smt` command (`/usr/sbin/smt`) may collide with the `smt` command from the `star` package (`/usr/bin/smt`). Either use the absolute path `/usr/sbin/smt`, create an alias, or set your `$PATH` accordingly.

Another solution is to always use the `smt-` *subcommand* syntax (connected with a minus sign) instead of `smt` *subcommand* (separated by a space).

7.1.2.1 smt-client

The `smt-client` command shows information about registered clients. The information includes:

- guid

- host name

- patch status

- time stamps of the patch status

- last contact with the SMT server

The **smt-client** understands the following options:

--verbose **or** -v

Show detailed information about the client. The last contact date is shown as well.

--debug **or** -d

Enable debugging mode.

--logfile **or** -L *file*

Specify the file the log will be written to.

--hostname **or** -h *name*

Only the entries whose host name begins with *name* will be listed.

--guid **or** -g *guid*

Only the entries whose GUID is *guid* will be listed.

--severity **or** -s *level*

Filter the result by the patch status information. The value *level* can be one of 'package-manager', 'security', 'recommended' or 'optional'. Only those entries are listed which have patches of the respective level.

7.1.2.2 smt-delete-registration

The **smt-delete-registration** command deletes one or more registrations from SMT and SUSE Customer Center. It will unregister machines from the system. The following options are available:

--guid *ID* **or** -g *ID*

Delete the machine with the guid *ID* from the system. You can use this option multiple times.

--debug **or** -d

Enable debugging mode.

7.1.2.3 smt-job

The **smt-job** script manages jobs for individual SMT clients. You can list, create, edit, or delete jobs with it. The following options are available:

--list or -l

List all client jobs. This is the default if the operation mode switch is omitted.

--verbose or -v *level*

Show detailed information about a job or jobs in a list mode. The *level* value can be a number from 0 to 3. The bigger the value, the more verbose the command is.

--create or -c

Create a new job.

--edit or -e

Edit an existing job.

--delete or -d

Delete an existing job.

--guid or -g *guid*

Specify the client's *guid*. This parameter can be used multiple times to create a job for more than one client.

--jobid or -j *id*

Specify the job ID. You need to specify job ID and client's *guid* when editing or deleting a job, because the same job for multiple clients has the same job ID.

--deleteall or -A *id*

Omit either the client's guid or the job ID in this delete operation. The missing parameter will match all respective jobs.

--type or -t *type*

Specify the job type. The type can be one of 'patchstatus', 'softwarepush', 'update', 'execute', 'reboot', 'wait', 'eject'. On the client, only 'patchstatus', 'softwarepush' and 'update' are enabled by default.

--description *description*

Specify a job description.

`--parent` *id*

> Specify the job ID of the parent job. Use it to describe a dependency. A job will not be processed until its parent has successfully finished.

`--name` **or** `-n` *name*

> Specify a job name.

`--persistent`

> Specify if a job is persistent. Non-persistent jobs are processed only once, while persistent jobs are processed again and again. Use `--timelag` to define the time that elapses until the next run.

`--finished`

> Search option for finished jobs.

`--targeted` *time*

> Specify the earliest execution time of a job. Note that the job most likely will not run exactly at that point in time, but probably some minutes or hours after. The reason is that the client polls in a fixed interval for jobs.

`--expires` *time*

> Define when the job will no longer be executed anymore.

`--timelag` *time*

> Define the time interval for persistent jobs.

For a complete list of possible options and their explanation, see the manual page of the smt-job command (**man** *smt-job*).

7.1.2.3.1 Examples

To list all finished jobs, enter the following:

```
smt-job --list --finished
```

To create a 'softwarepush' job that installs `xterm` and `bash` on client 12345 and 67890, enter the following:

```
smt-job --create -t softwarepush -P xterm -P bash -g 12345 -g 67890
```

To change the timing for a persistent job with job ID 42 and guid 12345 to run every 6 hours, enter the following:

```
smt-job --edit -j 42 -g 12345 --targeted 0000-00-00 --timelag 06:00:00
```

To delete all jobs with job ID 42, enter the following:

```
smt-job --delete -jobid 42 --deleteall
```

7.1.2.4   smt-list-products

The **smt-list-products** script lists all software products in the SMT database. The following options are available:

--used **or** -u
> Show only used products.

--catstat **or** -c
> Show whether all repositories needed for a product are locally mirrored.

7.1.2.5   smt-list-registrations

The **smt-list-registrations** script lists all registrations. There are two options available for this command.

--verbose **or** -v
> Show detailed information about the registered devices.

--format **or** -f *format*
> Format the output. Possible types of formats are *asciitable* and *csv*.

7.1.2.6   smt-mirror

The **smt-mirror** command performs the mirroring procedure and downloads repositories that are set to be mirrored.

You can run the **smt-mirror** with the following options:

--clean **or** -c
> Remove all files no longer mentioned in the metadata from the mirror. No mirroring occurs before cleanup.

--debug **or** -d
> Enable the debugging mode.

--deepverify
> Turn on verifying of all package checksums.

--hardlink *size*
> Search for duplicate files with a size greater than the size specified in kilobytes. Creates hard links for them.

--directory *path*
> Define the directory to work on. If you use this option, the default value configured in the smt.conf configuration file is ignored.

--dbreplfile *file*
> Define the path to the *.xml file to use as database replacement. You can create such a file with the **smt-scc** command.

--logfile *file* **or** -L *file*
> Specify the path to a log file.

7.1.2.7 smt-sync

The **smt-sync** or **smt sync** command gets data from SUSE Customer Center and updates the local SMT database. It can also save SUSE Customer Center data to a directory instead of the SMT database, or read the data from such a directory instead of downloading it from SUSE Customer Center itself.

For SUSE Linux Enterprise 11 clients, this script automatically decided whether Novell Customer Center or SUSE Customer Center would be used. Then **smt-ncc-sync** or **smt-scc-sync** was called, as appropriate. For SUSE Linux Enterprise 12 clients, only **smt-scc-sync** is supported.

7.1.2.8   smt-scc-sync

The **smt scc-sync** command gets data from the SUSE Customer Center and updates the local SMT database. It can also save SUSE Customer Center data to a directory instead of the SMT database, or read SUSE Customer Center data from a directory instead of downloading it from SUSE Customer Center itself.

You can run the **smt-scc-sync** with the following options:

--fromdir *directory*

Read SUSE Customer Center data from a directory instead of downloading it from SUSE Customer Center.

--todir *directory*

Write SUSE Customer Center data to the specified directory without updating the SMT database.

--createdbreplacementfile

Create a database replacement file for using **smt-mirror** without database.

--logfile *file* or -L *file*

Specify the path to a log file.

--debug

Enable debugging mode.

7.1.2.9   smt-register

The **smt-register** or **smt register** commands register all currently unregistered clients at the SUSE Customer Center. It also registers all clients whose data has changed since the last registration.

The following options are available:

--logfile *file* or -L *file*

Specify the path to a log file.

--debug

Enable debugging mode.

7.1.2.10 smt-report

The **smt-report** or **smt report** command generates a subscription report based on local calculation or SUSE Customer Center registrations.

The following options are available:

--mail **or** -m

> Activate mailing the report to the addresses configured with the SMT Server and written in /etc/smt.conf. The report will be rendered as tables.

--attach **or** -a

> Append the report to the e-mails in CSV format. This option should only be used together with the --mail option.

--quiet **or** -q

> Suppress output to STDOUT and runs **smt-report** in quiet mode.

--csv **or** -c

> The report will be exported to multiple files in CSV format. The first line of each *.csv file consists of the column names, then the data starts on line two. The --csv parameter should only be used together with the --file parameter. If the specified file name contains .csv as extension, the report format will be CSV (as if the --csv parameter was used).

--pdf **or** -p

> The report will be exported in PDF format. Use it only together with the -file option.

--xml

> The report will be exported in XML format. Use it only together with the -file option. For a detailed description of this XML format, see the manual page of the **smt-report** command.

--file **or** -F

> Export the report to one or several files. By default, the report will be written to a single file rendered as tables. Optionally, the file name or whole path may be specified after the parameter: --file *filename*. If no file name is specified, a default file name containing a time stamp is used. However, SMT will not check if the file or files already exist.
>
> In CSV mode the report will be written to multiple files, therefore the specified file name will expand to *[path/]filename-reportname.extension* for every report.

`--logfile` *filename* **or** `-L` *filename*

>   Specify path to a log file.

`--debug`

>   Enable debugging mode.

7.1.2.11   smt-repos

You can use **smt-repos** (or **smt repositories**) to list all available repositories and for enabling, disabling, or deleting repositories. The following options are available:

`--enable-mirror` **or** `-e`

>   Enable repository mirroring.

`--disable-mirror` **or** `-d`

>   Disable repository mirroring.

`--enable-by-prod` **or** `-p`

>   Enable repository mirroring by giving product data in the following format: `Product[,Version[,Architecture[,Release]]]`.

`--disable-by-prod` **or** `-P`

>   Disable repository mirroring by giving product data in the following format: `Product[,Version[,Architecture[,Release]]]`.

`--enable-staging` **or** `-s`

>   Enable repository staging.

`--disable-staging` **or** `-S`

>   Disable repository staging.

`--only-mirrorable` **or** `-m`

>   List only repositories that can be mirrored.

`--only-enabled` **or** `-o`

>   List only enabled repositories.

`--delete`

>   List repositories and delete them from disk.

`--namespace` *dirname*

>   Delete the repository in the specified name space.

`--verbose` **or** `-v`

>   Show detailed repository information.

7.1.2.12   smt-setup-custom-catalogs, smt-setup-custom-repos

The **smt-setup-custom-repos** or **smt setup-custom-repos** script is a tool to set up custom repositories (repositories not present in the download server) to be used with SMT. You can use this script to add a new repository to the SMT database or to delete a repository from the database. The script recognizes the following options:

`--productid`

>   ID of a product the repository belongs to. If a repository should belong to multiple products, use this option multiple times to assign the repository to all relevant products.

`--name`

>   The name of the custom repository.

`--description`

>   The description of the custom repository.

`--exturl`

>   The URL where this repository can be mirrored from. Only HTTP and HTTPS protocols are supported (no directory, file, or FTP).

`--delete`

>   Remove a custom repository with a given ID from the SMT database.

To set up a new repository, use the following command:

```
smt-setup-custom-repos --productid Product_ID \
--name Catalog_Name --exturl URL
```

For example:

```
smt-setup-custom-repos --productid 434 \
--name My_Catalog --exturl http://my.example.com/My_Catalog
```

To remove a configured repository, use the following command:

```
smt-setup-custom-repos --delete Catalog_ID
```

For example:

```
smt-setup-custom-repos --delete 1cf336d819e8e5904f4d4b05ee081971a0cc8afc
```

7.1.2.13　smt-staging

A *patch* is an update of a package or group of packages. The term *update* and *patch* are often interchangeable. With the **smt-staging** script, you can set up patch filters for update repositories. It can also help you generate both testing repositories and repositories for the production environment.

The first argument of **smt-staging** is always the *command*. It must be followed by a *repository*. The repository can be specified by *Name* and *Target* from the table scheme returned by the **smt-repos** command. Alternatively, it can be specified by its `Repository ID`, which is returned when running the commend **smt-repos -v**. The **smt-staging** script understands the following commands:

listupdates

> List available patches and their allowed/forbidden status.

allow/forbid

> Allow or forbid specified patches.

createrepo

> Generate both testing and production repository with allowed patches.

status

> Give information about both testing and production snapshots, and patch counts.

listgroups

> List staging groups.
>
> There is always one group available with the name "default". The default group has the path `repo/full`, `repo/testing` and `repo`. With creating a new group, new paths can be specified.

creategroup

> Create a staging group. Required parameters are: group name, testing directory name, and production directory name.

removegroup

> Remove a staging group. Required parameter is: group name.

The following options apply to any **smt-staging** command:

--logfile **or** -L *file path*

> Write log information to the specified file. If it does not exist, it is created.

--debug **or** -d

> Turn on the debugging output and log.

--verbose **or** -v

> Turn more detailed output on.

The following options apply to specific **smt-staging** commands:

--patch

> Specify a patch by its ID. You can get a list of available patches with the **listupates** command. This option can be used multiple times. Use it with the **allow**, **forbid**, and **listupdates** commands. If used with **listupdates**, the command will print detailed information about the specified patches.

--category

> Specify the patch category. The following categories are available: 'security', 'recommended' and 'optional'. Use it with the **allow**, **forbid**, and **listupdates** commands.

--all

> Allow or forbid all patches in the **allow** or **forbid** commands.

--individually

> Allow or forbid multiple patches (e.g. by category) one by one, that is, as if the --patch option had been used on each of the patches.

--testing

> Use with the **createrepo** command to generate a repository for testing. The repository will be generated from the full unfiltered local mirror of the remote repository. It will be written into the <MirrorTo>/repo/testing directory, where MirrorTo is the value taken from smt.conf.

`--production`

> Use with the **createrepo** command to generate a repository for production use. The repository will be generated from the testing repository. It will be written into the `<MirrorTo>/repo` directory, where `MirrorTo` is the value taken from `smt.conf`. If the testing repository does not exist, the production repository will be generated from the full unfiltered local mirror of the remote repository.

`--group`

> Specify on which group the command should work. The default for `--group` is the name `default`.

`--nohardlink`

> During the repository creation with the **createrepo** command, avoid creating hard links instead of copying files. If not specified, hard links are created instead.

`--nodesc`

> Do not print patch descriptions and summaries—to save some screen space and make the output more readable.

`--sort-by-version`

> Sort the `listupdates` table by patch version. The higher the version, the newer the patch should be.

`--sort-by-category`

> Sort the `listupdates` table by patch category.

7.1.2.14   smt-support

The **smt-support** command manages uploaded support data usually coming from the **supportconfig** tool. You can forward the data to SUSE, either selectively or in full. This command understands the following options:

`--incoming` **or** `-i directory`

> Specify the directory where the supportconfig archives are uploaded. You can also set this option with the `SMT_INCOMING` environment variable. The default `SMT_INCOMING` directory is `/var/spool/smt-support`.

`--list` **or** `-l`

> List the uploaded supportconfig archives in the incoming directory.

`--remove` **or** `-r` *archive*

>   Delete the specified archive.

`--empty` **or** `-R`

>   Delete all archives in the incoming directory.

`--upload` **or** `-u` *archive*

>   Upload the specified archive to SUSE. If you specify `-s`, `-n`, `-c`, `-p`, and `-e` options, the archive is repackaged with contact information.

`--uploadall` **or** `-U`

>   Upload all archives in the incoming directory to SUSE.

`--srnum` **or** `-s` *SR number*

>   Accept the Novell Service Request 11-digit number.

`--name` **or** `-n` *name*

>   Enter the first and last name of the contact, in quotes.

`--company` **or** `-c` *company*

>   Enter the company name.

`--storeid` **or** `-d` *id*

>   Enter the store ID, if applicable.

`--terminalid` **or** `-t` *id*

>   Enter the terminal ID, if applicable.

`--phone` **or** `-p` *phone*

>   Enter the phone number of the contact person.

`--email` **or** `-e` *email*

>   Enter the e-mail address of the contact.

7.1.3   SMT `systemd` Commands

You can operate SMT related services with the standard `systemd` commands:

`systemctl start smt.target`

>   Start the SMT services.

systemctl stop smt.target

> Stop the SMT services.

systemctl status smt.target

> Check the status of the SMT services. Checks whether httpd, MariaDB, and cron are running.

systemctl restart smt.target

> Restart the SMT services.

systemctl try-restart smt.target

> Check whether the SMT services are enabled and if so, restart them.

You can enable and disable SMT with the YaST SMT Server module.

7.2 SMT Configuration Files

The main SMT configuration file is `/etc/smt.conf`. You can set most of the options with the YaST SMT Server module. Another important configuration file is `/etc/smt.d/smt-cron.conf`, which contains parameters for commands launched as SMT scheduled jobs.

7.2.1 /etc/smt.conf

The `/etc/smt.conf` file has several sections. The `[NU]` section contains the update credentials and URL. The `[DB]` section contains the configuration of the MySQL database for SMT. The `[LOCAL]` section includes other configuration data. The `[REPORT]` section contains the configuration of SMT reports.

 Warning

> The `/etc/smt.conf` file contains passwords in clear text, and its default permissions (640, root, wwwrun) make its content easily accessible with scripts running on the Apache server. Be careful with running other software on the SMT Apache server. The best policy is to use this server only for SMT.

7.2.1.1 [NU] Section of /etc/smt.conf

The following options are available in the [NU] section:

NUUrl

> URL of the update service. Usually it should contain the `https://updates.suse.com/`
> URL.

NURegUrl

> URL of the update registration service. It is used by **smt-sync**. If this option is missing,
> the URL from `/etc/SUSEConnect` is used as a fallback.

NUUser

> `NUUser` should contain the user name for update service. For information about getting
> organization credentials, see *Section 3.1, "Mirroring Credentials"*. You can set this value with
> the SMT Server.

NUPass

> `NUPass` is the password for the user defined in `NUUser`. For information about getting
> organization credentials, see *Section 3.1, "Mirroring Credentials"*. You can set this value with
> the SMT Server.

ApiType

> `ApiType` is the type of service SMT uses; it can be either `NCC` for Novell Customer Center
> or `SCC` for SUSE Customer Center. The only supported value for SMT 12 is `SCC`.

7.2.1.2 [DB] Section of /etc/smt.conf

The three options defined in the [DB] section are used for configuring the database for SMT.
Currently, only MySQL is supported by SMT.

config

> The first parameter of the DBI->connect Perl method used for connection to the MySQL
> database. The value should be in the form
>
> ```
> dbi:mysql:database=smt;host=localhost
> ```
>
> where *smt* is the name of the database and *localhost* is the host name of the database
> server.

user

The user for the database. The default value is `smt`.

pass

The password for the database user. You can set the password with the YaST SMT Server module.

7.2.1.3   [LOCAL] Section of /etc/smt.conf

The following options are available in the `[LOCAL]` section:

url

The base URL of the SMT server which is used to construct URLs of the repositories available on the server. This value should be set by YaST automatically during installation. The format of this option should be: `https://server.domain.tld/`.

You can change the URL manually. For example, the administrator may choose to use the `http://` scheme instead of `https://` for performance reasons. Another reason may be using an alias (configured with CNAME in DNS) instead of the host name of the server, for example `http://smt.domain.tld/` instead of `http://server1.domain.tld/`.

nccEmail

E-mail address used for registration at the SUSE Customer Center. The SMT administrator can set this value with the YaST SMT Server module.

MirrorTo

Determines the path to mirror to.

MirrorAll

If the `MirrorAll` option is set to `true`, the **smt-sync** script will set all repositories that can be mirrored to be mirrored (DOMIRROR flag).

MirrorSRC

If the `MirrorSRC` option is set to `true`, source RPM packages are mirrored.

 Note: Default Value Changed with SMT 11 SP2

With SMT 11 SP2, the preset default value was changed to `false`. If you also want SMT to mirror source RPM packages on new installations, set `MirrorSRC` to `true`. Upgraded systems are not affected.

forwardRegistration

> For SMT 11, this option determined whether the clients registered at SMT should be registered at Novell Customer Center, too. This option does not work with SUSE Customer Center yet.

rndRegister

> Specify a delay in seconds before the clients are registered at SUSE Customer Center. The value is a random number between `0` and `450`, generated by the YaST SMT Server module. The purpose of this random delay is to prevent a high load on the SUSE Customer Center server that would occur if all smt-register cron jobs connected at the same time.

mirror_preunlock_hook

> Specify the path to the script that will be run before the **smt-mirror** script removes its lock.

mirror_postunlock_hook

> Specify the path to the script that will be run after the **smt-mirror** script removes its lock.

HTTPProxy

> If you do not want to use global proxy settings, specify the proxy to be used for HTTP connection here. Use the following form: `http://proxy.example.com:3128`.
>
> If the proxy settings are not configured in `/etc/smt.conf`, the global proxy settings configured in `/etc/syconfig/proxy` are used. You can configure the global proxy settings with the YaST Proxy module.

HTTPSProxy

> If you do not want to use global proxy settings, specify the proxy to be used for HTTPS connection here. Use the form: `https://proxy.example.com:3128`.
>
> If the proxy settings are not configured in `/etc/smt.conf`, the global proxy settings configured in `/etc/syconfig/proxy` are used. You can configure the global proxy settings with the YaST Proxy module.

ProxyUser

> If your proxy requires authentication, specify a user name and password here, using the `username:password` format.
>
> If the proxy settings are not configured in `/etc/smt.conf`, the global proxy settings configured in `/etc/syconfig/proxy` are used. You can configure the global proxy settings with the YaST Proxy module.

Tip: Global User Authentication Setting

If you configure the global proxy settings with YaST, manually copy /root/.curlrc to the home directory of the smt and adjust the permissions with the following commands as root:

```
cp /root/.curlrc /var/lib/smt/
chown smt:www /var/lib/smt/.curlrc
```

requiredAuthType

Specify an authentication type to access the repository. There are three possible types:

- none - no authentication is required. This is the default value.

- lazy - only user name and password are checked. A valid user can access all repositories.

- strict - checks also if the user has access to the repository.

smtUser

Specify a user name of a Unix user under which all smt commands will run.

signingKeyID

Specify the ID of the GPG key to sign modified repositories. The user specified under smtUser needs to have access to the key. If this option is not set, the modified repositories will be unsigned.

7.2.1.4 [REST] Section of /etc/smt.conf

The following options are available in the [REST] section:

enableRESTAdminAccess

If set to *1*, turns administrative access to the SMT RESTService on. Default value is *0*.

RESTAdminUser

Specify the user name that the REST-Admin uses to log in. Default value is *RESTroot*.

RESTAdminPassword

Specify the password for the REST-Admin user. The option has no default value. An empty password is invalid.

7.2.1.5 [JOBQUEUE] Section of /etc/smt.conf

The following options are available in the `[JOBQUEUE]` section:

`maxFinishedJobAge`

Specify the maximum age of finished non-persistent jobs in days. Default value is 8.

`jobStatusIsSuccess`

Specify a comma separated list of JobQueue status IDs that should be interpreted as successful. For more information about possible status IDs, see **smt-job --help**. Leaving this option empty is interpreted as default (1,4).

7.2.1.6 [REPORT] Section of /etc/smt.conf

The following options are available in the `[REPORT]` section:

`reportEmail`

A comma separated list of e-mail addresses to send SMT status reports to. You can set this list with the YaST SMT Server module.

`reportEmailFrom`

`From` field of report e-mails. If not set, the default `root@hostname.domainname` will be used.

`mailServer`

Relay mail server. If empty, e-mails are sent directly.

`mailServerPort`

Port of the relay mail server set in `mailServer`.

`mailServerUser`

User name for authentication to the mail server set in `mailServer`.

`mailServerPassword`

Password for authentication to the mail server set in `mailServer`.

7.2.1.7 Example /etc/smt.conf

EXAMPLE 7.1: SMT.CONF

```
[NU]
```

```
NUUrl=https://updates.suse.com/
NURegUrl=https://scc.suse.com/connect
NUUser = exampleuser
NUPass = examplepassword
ApiType = SCC


[DB]
config = dbi:mysql:database=smt;host=localhost
user = smt
pass = smt


[LOCAL]
# Default should be http://server.domain.top/
url = http://smt.example.com/
# This email address is used for registration at SCC
nccEmail = exampleuser@example.com
MirrorTo = /srv/www/htdocs
MirrorAll = false
MirrorSRC = false
forwardRegistration = true
rndRegister = 127
# The hook script that should be called before the smt-mirror script removes its
 lock
mirror_preunlock_hook =
# The hook script that should be called after the smt-mirror script removed its lock
mirror_postunlock_hook =
# specify proxy settings here, if you do not want to use the global proxy settings
# If you leave these options empty the global options are used.
#
# specify which proxy you want to use for HTTP connection
# in the form http://proxy.example.com:3128
HTTPProxy =
# specify which proxy you want to use for HTTPS connection
# in the form http://proxy.example.com:3128
HTTPSProxy =
# specify username and password if your proxy requires authentication
```

```
# in the form username:password
ProxyUser =
#
# require authentication to access the repository?
# Three possible authtypes can be configured here
# 1) none   : no authentication required (default)
# 2) lazy   : check only username and password. A valid user has access to all
  repositories
# 3) strict : check also if this user has access to the repository.
#
requiredAuthType = none
#
# the smt commands should run with this unix user
#
smtUser = smt
#
# ID of the GPG key to be used to sign modified (filtered) repositories.
# The key must be accessible by the user who runs SMT, i.e. the user specified
# in the 'smtUser' configuration option.
#
# If empty, the modified repositories will be unsigned.
#
signingKeyID =
#
# This string is sent in HTTP requests as UserAgent.
# If the key UserAgent does not exist, a default is used.
# If UserAgent is empty, no UserAgent string is set.
#
#UserAgent=
# Organization credentials for this SMT server.
# These are currently only used to get list of all available repositories
# from https://your.smt.url/repo/repoindex.xml
# Note: if authenticated as a client machine instead of these mirrorUser,
# the above URL returns only repositories relevant for that client.
mirrorUser =
mirrorPassword =
```

```
[REST]
# Enable administrative access to the SMT RESTService by setting
 enableRESTAdminAccess=1
# default: 0
enableRESTAdminAccess = 0
# Define the username the REST-Admin uses for login
# default: RESTroot
RESTAdminUser = RESTroot
# Define the password for the REST-Admin (note: empty password is invalid)
# default: <empty>
RESTAdminPassword =


[JOBQUEUE]
# maximum age of finished (non-persistent) jobs in days
# default: 8
maxFinishedJobAge = 8
# comma separated list of JobQueue status IDs that should be interpreted as
 successful
# See smt-job --help for more information about possible Status IDs
# Please note: An empty string will be interpreted as default (1,4).
# default: 1,4
# useful:  1,4,6
jobStatusIsSuccess = 1,4


[REPORT]
# comma separated list of eMail addresses where the status reports will be sent to
reportEmail = exampleuser@example.com
# from field of report mails - if empty it defaults to
 "root@<hostname>.<domainname>"
reportEmailFrom =
# relay mail server - leave empty if mail should be sent directly
mailServer =
mailServerPort =
# mail server authentication - leave empty if not required
mailServerUser =
```

/etc/smt.conf

```
mailServerPassword =
```

7.2.2 /etc/smt.d/smt-cron.conf

The `/etc/smt.d/smt-cron.conf` configuration file contains options of the SMT commands launched as SMT scheduled jobs set with YaST (see *Section 2.5, "Setting the SMT Job Schedule with YaST"*). Cron is used to launch these scheduled jobs. The cron table is located in the `/etc/cron.d/novell.com-smt` file.

SCC_SYNC_PARAMS

> Contains parameters of the **smt scc-sync** command, if called as part of an SMT scheduled job via cron. The default value is `"-L /var/log/smt/smt-sync.log --mail"`.

MIRROR_PARAMS

> Contains parameters of the **smt mirror** command, if called as part of an SMT scheduled job via cron. The default value is `"-L /var/log/smt/smt-mirror.log --mail"` .

REGISTER_PARAMS

> Contains parameters of the **smt register** command, if called as part of an SMT scheduled job via cron. The default value is `"-r -L /var/log/smt/smt-register.log --mail"` .

REPORT_PARAMS

> Contains parameters of the **smt report** command, if called as part of an SMT scheduled job via cron. The default value is `"--mail --attach -L /var/log/smt/smt-report.log"` .

JOBQUEUECLEANUP_PARAMS

> Contains parameters for smt jobqueue cleanup, if called as a part of an SMT scheduled job via cron. The default value is `"--mail -L /var/log/smt/smt-jobqueuecleanup.log"`.

7.3 Server Certificates

For communication between the SMT server and client machines, the encrypted HTTPS protocol is used, requiring a server certificate. If the certificate is not available, or if clients are not configured to use the certificate, the communication between server and clients will fail.

Every client must be able to verify the server certificate by trusting the CA (certificate authority) certificate that signed the server certificate. Therefore, the SMT server provides a copy of the CA at `/srv/www/htdocs/smt.crt`. This CA can be downloaded from every client via the URL `http://FQDN/smt.crt`. The copy is created when YaST writes the SMT configuration. Whenever SMT is started with **systemctl start smt.target**, it checks the certificate. If a new CA certificate exists, it is copied again. Therefore, whenever the CA certificate is changed, restart SMT using the **systemctl restart smt.target** command.

When the SMT Server module applies configuration changes, it checks for the existence of the common server certificate. If the certificate does not exist, YaST asks whether the certificate should be created. If the user confirms, the YaST CA Management module is started.

7.3.1   Certificate Expiration

The common server certificate SMT uses is valid for one year. After that time, a new certificate is needed. Either generate a new certificate using YaST CA Management module or import a new certificate using the YaST Common Server Certificate module. Both options are described in the following sections.

As long as the same CA certificate is used, there is no need to update certificates on the client machines. The generated CA certificate is valid for 10 years.

7.3.2   Creating a New Common Server Certificate

To create a new common server certificate with YaST, proceed as follows:

1. Start YaST and select *Security and Users* › *CA Management*. Alternatively, start the YaST CA Management module from a command line by entering **yast2 ca_mgm** as root.

2. Select the required CA and click *Enter CA*.

3. Enter the password if entering a CA for the first time. YaST displays the CA key information in the *Description* tab.

4. Click the *Certificates* tab (see *Figure 7.1, "Certificates of a CA"*) and select *Add* › *Add Server Certificate*.

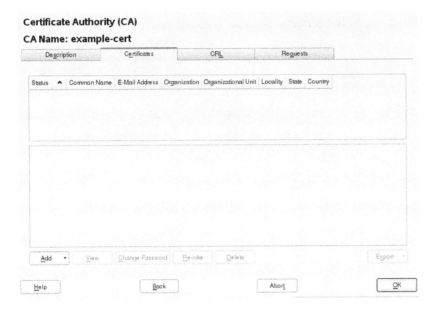

FIGURE 7.1: CERTIFICATES OF A CA

5. Enter the fully qualified domain name of the server as *Common Name*. Add a valid e-mail address of the server administrator. Other fields, such as *Organization*, *Organizational Unit*, *Locality*, and *State* are optional. Click *Next* to proceed.

 Important: Host Name in Server Certificate

The server certificate must contain the correct host name. If the client requests server `https://some.hostname/`, then `some.hostname` must be part of the certificate. The host name must either be used as the *Common Name*, see *Step 5*, or as the *Subject Alternative Name*, see *Step 7*: `DNS:some.hostname` and `IP:<ipaddress>`.

6. Enter a *Password* for the private key of the certificate and re-enter it in the next field to verify it.

7. If you want to define a *Subject Alternative Name*, click *Advanced Options*, select *Subject Alternative Name* from the list and click *Add*.

8. If you want to keep the default values for the other options, like *Key Length* and *Valid Period*, click *Next*. An overview of the certificate to be created is shown.

9. Click *Create* to generate the certificate.

10. To export the new certificate as the common server certificate, select it in the *Certificates* tab and select *Export › Export as Common Server Certificate.*

11. After having created a new certificate, restart SMT using the `systemctl restart smt.target` command. Restarting SMT ensures that the new certificate is copied from `/etc/ssl/certs/YaST-CA.pem` to `/srv/www/htdocs/smt.crt`, the copy SMT uses. Restarting SMT also restarts the Web server.

For detailed information about managing certification and further usage of the YaST CA Management module and the Common Server Certificate module, refer to the *Security Guide* coming with the base system.

7.3.3 Importing a Common Server Certificate

You can import an own common server certificate from a file. The certificate to be imported needs to be in the PKCS12 format with CA chain. Common server certificates can be imported with the YaST Common Server Certificate module.

To import an own certificate with YaST, proceed as follows:

1. Start YaST and select *Security and Users › Common Server Certificate.* Alternatively, start the YaST Common Server Certificate module from the command line by entering `yast2 common_cert` as `root`.
   The description of the currently used common server certificate is shown in the dialog that opens.

2. Click *Import* and select the file containing the certificate to be imported. Specify the certificate password in the *Password* field.

3. Press *Next.* If the certificate is successfully imported, close YaST with *Finish.*

4. After having created a new certificate, restart SMT using the `systemctl restart smt.target` command. Restarting SMT ensures that the new certificate is copied from `/etc/ssl/certs/YaST-CA.pem` to `/srv/www/htdocs/smt.crt`, the copy SMT uses. Restarting SMT also restarts the Web server.

7.3.4 Synchronizing Time between SMT Server and Clients

The synchronization of time between the SMT server and clients is highly recommended. Each server certificate has a validity period. If the client happens to be set to a time outside of this period, the certificate validation on the client side fails.

Therefore, it is advisable to keep the time on the server and clients synchronized. You can easily synchronize the time using NTP (network time protocol). Use **yast2 ntp-client** to configure an NTP client. Find detailed information about NTP in the *Administration Guide*.

8 Configuring Clients to Use SMT

Any machine running SUSE Linux Enterprise 10 SP4, 11 SP1 or later, or any version of SUSE Linux Enterprise 12 can be configured to register against SMT and download software updates from there, instead of communicating directly with SUSE Customer Center or Novell Customer Center.

If your network includes an SMT server to provide a local update source, you need to equip the client with the server's URL. As client and server communicate via the HTTPS protocol during registration, you also need to make sure the client trusts the server's certificate. In case you set up your SMT server to use the default server certificate, the CA certificate will be available on the SMT server at `http://FQDN/smt.crt` .

If the certificate is not issued by a well-trusted authority, the registration process will import the certificate from the URL specified as `regcert` parameter (SLES 10 and 11), or, for SLE 12, the certificate will be downloaded automatically from SMT. In this case, the client displays the new certificate details (its fingerprint), and you need to accept the certificate.

There are several ways to provide the registration information and to configure the client machine to use SMT:

1. Provide the required information via kernel parameters at boot time (*Section 8.1, "Using Kernel Parameters to Access an SMT Server"*).

2. Configure the clients using an AutoYaST profile (*Section 8.2, "Configuring Clients with AutoYaST Profile"*).

3. Use the `clientSetup4SMT.sh` script (*Section 8.3, "Configuring Clients with the clientSetup4SMT.sh Script in SLE 11 and 12"*). This script can be run on a client to make it register against a specified SMT server.

4. In SUSE Linux Enterprise 11 and 12, you can set the SMT server URL with the YaST registration module during installation (*Section 8.4, "Configuring Clients with YaST"*).

These methods are described in the following sections.

8.1 Using Kernel Parameters to Access an SMT Server

 Important

Note that the `regcert` kernel boot parameter is supported for SLE 10 and 11. It is not supported for SLE 12.

Any client can be configured to use SMT by providing the following kernel parameters during machine boot: `regurl` and `regcert`. The first parameter is mandatory, the latter is optional.

 Warning: Beware of Typing Errors

Make sure the values you enter are correct. If `regurl` has not been specified correctly, the registration of the update source will fail.

If an invalid value for `regcert` has been entered, you will be prompted for a local path to the certificate. In case `regcert` is not specified , it will default to `http://FQDN/smt.crt` with `FQDN` being the name of the SMT server.

regurl

URL of the SMT server.

For SLE 11 and older clients, the URL needs to be in the following format: `https://FQDN/center/regsvc/` with `FQDN` being the fully qualified host name of the SMT server. It must be identical to the FQDN of the server certificate used on the SMT server. Example:

```
regurl=https://smt.example.com/center/regsvc/
```

For SLE 12 clients, the URL needs to be in the following format: `https://FQDN/connect/` with `FQDN` being the fully qualified host name of the SMT server. It must be identical to the FQDN of the server certificate used on the SMT server. Example:

```
regurl=https://smt.example.com/connect/
```

regcert

Location of the SMT server's CA certificate. Specify one of the following locations:

URL

> Remote location (http, https or ftp) from which the certificate can be downloaded. Example:

```
regcert=http://smt.example.com/smt.crt
```

Floppy

> Specifies a location on a floppy. The floppy needs to be inserted at boot time—you will not be prompted to insert it if it is missing. The value has to start with the string `floppy`, followed by the path to the certificate. Example:

```
regcert=floppy/smt/smt-ca.crt
```

Local Path

> Absolute path to the certificate on the local machine. Example:

```
regcert=/data/inst/smt/smt-ca.cert
```

Interactive

> Use `ask` to open a pop-up menu during installation where you can specify the path to the certificate. Do not use this option with AutoYaST. Example:

```
regcert=ask
```

Deactivate Certificate Installation

> Use `done` if either the certificate will be installed by an add-on product, or if you are using a certificate issued by an official certificate authority. Example:

```
regcert=done
```

Warning: Change of SMT Server Certificate

If the SMT server gets a new certificate from an untrusted CA, the clients need to retrieve the new CA certificate file.

On SLE 10 and 11, this is done automatically with the registration process but only if a URL was used at installation time to retrieve the certificate, or if the `regcert` parameter was omitted and thus the default URL is used. If the certificate was loaded using any other method, such as floppy or local path, the CA certificate will not be updated.

On SLES 12, after the certificate has changed, YaST displays a dialog window for importing a new certificate. If you confirm importing the new certificate, the old one is replaced with the new one.

8.2   Configuring Clients with AutoYaST Profile

Clients can be configured to register with SMT server via AutoYaST profile. For general information about creating AutoYaST profiles and preparing automatic installation, refer to the *AutoYaST Guide*. In this section, only SMT specific configuration is described.

To configure SMT specific data using AutoYaST, follow the steps for the relevant version of SMT client.

8.2.1   Configuring SUSE Linux Enterprise 11 Clients

1. As `root`, start YaST and select *Miscellaneous* › *Autoinstallation* to start the graphical AutoYaST front-end.
   From a command line, you can start the graphical AutoYaST front-end with the **yast2 autoyast** command.

2. Open an existing profile using *File* › *Open*, create a profile based on the current system's configuration using *Tools* › *Create Reference Profile*, or work with an empty profile.

3. Select *Software* › *Novell Customer Center Configuration*. An overview of the current configuration is shown.

4. Click *Configure*.

5. Set the URL of the *SMT Server* and, optionally, the location of the *SMT Certificate*. The possible values are the same as for the kernel parameters `regurl` and `regcert` (see *Section 8.1, "Using Kernel Parameters to Access an SMT Server"*). The only exception is that the `ask` value for `regcert` does not work in AutoYaST, because it requires user interaction. If using it, the registration process will be skipped.

6. Perform all other configuration needed for the systems to be deployed.

7. Select *File > Save As* and enter a file name for the profile, such as `autoinst.xml`.

8.2.2 Configuring SUSE Linux Enterprise 12 Clients

1. As `root`, start YaST and select *Miscellaneous > Autoinstallation* to start the graphical AutoYaST front-end.
From a command line, you can start the graphical AutoYaST front-end with the **yast2 autoyast** command.

2. Open an existing profile using *File > Open*, create a profile based on the current system's configuration using *Tools > Create Reference Profile*, or work with an empty profile.

3. Select *Software > Product Registration*. An overview of the current configuration is shown.

4. Click *Edit*.

5. Check *Register the Product*, set the URL of the SMT server in *Use Specific Server URL Instead of the Default*, and you can set the *Optional SSL Server Certificate URL*. The possible values for the server URL are the same as for the kernel parameter `regurl`. For the SSL certificate location, you can use either HTTP or HTTPS based URLs.

6. Perform all other configuration needed for the systems to be deployed, then click *Finish* to return to the main screen.

7. Select *File > Save As* and enter a file name for the profile, such as `autoinst.xml`.

8.3 Configuring Clients with the clientSetup4SMT.sh Script in SLE 11 and 12

In SLE 11 and 12, the **/usr/share/doc/packages/smt/clientSetup4SMT.sh** script is provided together with SMT. This script allows you to configure a client machine to use an SMT server. It can also be used to reconfigure an existing client to use a different SMT server.

 Note: Installation of wget

The script `clientSetup4SMT.sh` itself uses **wget**, so **wget** must be installed on the client.

To configure a client machine to use SMT with the **clientSetup4SMT.sh** script, follow these steps:

1. Copy the `clientSetup4SMT.sh` script from your SMT server to the client machine. The script is available at `<SMT_HOSTNAME>/repo/tools/clientSetup4SMT.sh` and `/srv/www/htdocs/repo/tools/clientSetup4SMT.sh`. You can download it with a browser, using **wget**, or by another means, such as with **scp**.

2. As `root`, execute the script on the client machine. The script can be executed in two ways. In the first case, the script name is followed by the registration URL; for example:

   ```
   ./clientSetup4SMT.sh https://smt.example.com/center/regsvc
   ```

   In the second case, the script uses the `--host` option followed by the host name of the SMT server, and `--regcert` followed by the URL of the SSL certificate; for example:

   ```
   ./clientSetup4SMT.sh --host smt.example.com \
     --regcert http://smt.example.com/certs/smt.crt
   ```

   In this case, without any "namespace" specified, the client will be configured to use the default production repositories. If `--namespace groupname` is specified, the client will use that staging group.

3. The script downloads the server's CA certificate. Accept it by pressing ⓨ.

4. The script performs all necessary modifications on the client. However, the registration itself is not performed by the script.

5. The script downloads and asks to accept additional GPG keys to sign repositories with.

6. On SLE 11, perform the registration by executing **suse_register** or running the **yast2 inst_suse_register** module on the client.
   On SLE 12, perform the registration by executing

```
SUSEConnect -p product_name --url https://smt.example.org
```

   or running the **yast2 registration** (SLES 12 SP1) or **yast2 scc** (SLES 12) module on the client.

The **clientSetup4SMT.sh** script works with SUSE Linux Enterprise 10 SP2 and later SPs, SLE 11, and SLE 12 systems.

This script is also provided for download. You can get it by calling:

`wget http://smt.example.com/repo/tools/clientSetup4SMT.sh`

8.3.1 Problems Downloading GPG Keys from the Server

The `apache2-example-pages` package includes a `robots.txt` file. The file is installed into the Apache2 document root directory, and controls how clients can access files from the Web server. If this package is installed on the server, `clientSetup4SMT.sh` fails to download the keys stored under `/repo/keys`.

You can solve this problem by either editing `robots.txt`, or uninstalling the `apache2-example-ple-pages` package.

If you choose to edit the `robots.txt` file, add before the `Disallow: /` statement:

```
Allow: /repo/keys
```

8.4 Configuring Clients with YaST

8.4.1 Configuring Clients with YaST in SLE 11

To configure a client to perform the registration against an SMT server use the YaST registration module (`yast2 inst_suse_register`).

Click *Advanced* › *Local Registration Server* and enter the name of the SMT server plus the path to the registration internals (`/center/regsvc/`), e.g.:

```
https://smt.example.com/center/regsvc/
```

After confirmation the certificate is loaded and the user is asked to accept it. Then continue.

 Warning: Staging Groups Registration

If a staging group is used, make sure that settings in `/etc/suseRegister.conf` are done accordingly. If not already done, modify the `register=` parameter and append `&namespace=namespace`. For more information about staging groups, see *Section 4.3, "Staging Repositories"*.

Alternatively, use the **clientSetup4SMT.sh** script (see *Section 8.3, "Configuring Clients with the clientSetup4SMT.sh Script in SLE 11 and 12"*).

8.4.2 Configuring Clients with YaST in SLE 12

To configure a client to perform the registration against an SMT server use the YaST *Product Registration* module **yast2 registration** (SLES 12 SP1) or **yast2 scc** (SLES 12).

On the client, the credentials are not necessary and you may leave the relevant fields empty. Click *Local Registration Server* and enter its URL. Then click *Next* until the exit from the module.

8.5 Registering SLE11 Clients against SMT Test Environment

To configure a client to register against the test environment instead of the production environment, modify `/etc/suseRegister.conf` on the client machine by setting:

```
register = command=register&namespace=testing
```

For more information about using SMT with a test environment, see *Section 3.5, "Using the Test Environment"*.

8.6 Registering SLE12 Clients against SMT Test Environment

To configure a client to register against the test environment instead of the production environment, modify `/etc/SUSEConnect` on the client machine by setting:

```
namespace: testing
```

For more information about using SMT with a test environment, see *Section 3.5, "Using the Test Environment"*.

8.7 Listing Accessible Repositories

To retrieve the accessible repositories for a client, download `repo/repoindex.xml` from the SMT server with the client's credentials. The credentials are stored in `/etc/zypp/credentials.d/SCCcredentials` (SLES 12) or `/etc/zypp/credentials.d/NCCcredentials` (SLES 11) on the client machine. Using **wget**, the command for testing could be as follows:

```
wget https://USER:PASS@smt.example.com/repo/repoindex.xml
```

`repoindex.xml` returns the complete repository list as they come from the vendor. If a repository is marked for staging, `repoindex.xml` lists the repository in the `full` namespace (`repos/full/$RCE`).

To get a list of all repositories available on the SMT server, use the credentials specified in the `[LOCAL]` section of `/etc/smt.conf` on the server as `mirrorUser` and `mirrorPassword`.

8.8 Online Migration of SUSE Linux Enterprise Clients

SUSE Linux Enterprise clients registered against SMT can be migrated online to the latest service pack of the same major release the same way as clients registered against SUSE Customer Center or Novell Customer Center. Before starting the migration, make sure that SMT is configured to provide the correct version of repositories to which you need the clients to migrate.

For detailed information on online migration, see https://www.suse.com/documentation/sles11/book_sle_deployment/data/cha_update_sle.html for SUSE Linux Enterprise 11 clients, or *Book "Deployment Guide", Chapter 14 "Upgrading SUSE Linux Enterprise"* for SUSE Linux Enterprise 12 clients.

8.9 How to Update Red Hat Enterprise Linux with SMT

SMT enables customers that possess the required entitlements to mirror updates for Red Hat Enterprise Linux (RHEL). Refer to http://www.suse.com/products/expandedsupport/ for details on SUSE Linux Enterprise Server Subscription with Expanded Support. This section discusses the actions required to configure the SMT server and clients (RHEL servers) for this solution.

 Note: SUSE Linux Enterprise Server 10

Configuring RHEL client with Subscription Management Tool for SUSE Linux Enterprise (SMT 1.0) running SUSE Linux Enterprise Server 10 is slightly different. For more information, see How to update Red Hat Enterprise Linux with SMT. [http://www.novell.com/support/search.do?usemicrosite=true&searchString=7001751]

8.9.1 How to Prepare SMT Server for Mirroring and Publishing Updates for RHEL

1. Install SUSE Linux Enterprise Server (SLES) with the SMT packages as per the documentation on the respective products.

2. During SMT setup, use organization credentials that have access to Novell-provided RHEL update catalogs.

3. Verify that the organization credentials have access to download updates for the Red Hat products with

```
smt-repos -m | grep RES
```

4. Enable mirroring of the RHEL update catalog(s) for the desired architecture(s):

```
smt-repos -e repo-name architecture
```

5. Mirror the updates and log verbose output:

```
smt-mirror -d -L /var/log/smt/smt-mirror.log
```

The updates for RHEL will also be mirrored automatically as part of the default nightly SMT mirroring cron job. When the mirror process of the catalogs for your RHEL products has completed, the updates are available via

```
http://smt-server.your-domain.top/repo/$RCE/catalog-name/architecture/
```

6. To enable GPG checking of the repositories, the key used to sign the repositories needs to be made available to the RHEL clients. This key is now available in the res-signingkeys package, which is included in the SMT 11 installation source.

   - Install the `res-signingkeys` package with the command

     ```
     zypper in -y res-signingkeys
     ```

   - The installation of the package stores the key file as `/srv/www/htdocs/repo/keys/res-signingkeys.key`.

   - Now the key is available to the clients and can be imported into their RPM database as described later.

8.9.2   How to Configure the YUM Client on RHEL 5.2 to Receive Updates from SMT

1. Import the repository signing key downloaded above into the local RPM database with

```
rpm --import http://smt-server.domain.top/repo/keys/res-signingkeys.key
```

2. Create a file in `/etc/yum.repos.d/` and name it `RES5.repo`.

3. Edit the file and enter the repository data, and point to the catalog on the SMT server as follows:

```
[smt]
name=SMT repository
baseurl=http://smt-server.domain.top/repo/$RCE/catalog-name/architecture/
enabled=1
gpgcheck=1
```

Example of base URL:

```
http://smt.mycompany.com/repo/$RCE/RES5/i386/
```

4. Save the file.

5. Disable standard Red Hat repositories by setting

```
enabled=0
```

in the repository entries in other files in `/etc/yum.repos.d/` (if any are enabled). Both YUM and the update notification applet should work correctly now and notify of available updates when applicable. You may need to restart the applet.

8.9.3   How to Configure the UP2DATE Client on RHEL 3.9 and 4.7 to Receive Updates from SMT

1. Import the repository signing key downloaded above into the local RPM database with

```
rpm --import http://smt-server.domain.top/repo/keys/res-signingkeys.key
```

2. Edit the file `/etc/sysconfig/rhn/sources` and make the following changes:

3. Comment out any lines starting with `up2date`.

Normally, there will be a line that says "up2date default".

4. Add an entry pointing to the SMT repository (all in one line):

```
yum repo-name http://smt-server.domain.top/repo/$RCE/catalog-name/architecture/
```

where `repo-name` should be set to RES3 for 3.9 and RES4 for 4.7.

5. Save the file.

Both up2date and the update notification applet should work correctly now, pointing to the SMT repository and indicating updates when available. In case of trouble, try to restart the applet.

To ensure correct reporting of the Red Hat Enterprise systems in SUSE Customer Center, they need to be registered against your SMT server. For this a special suseRegisterRES package is provided through the RES* catalogs and it should be installed, configured and executed as described below.

8.9.4 How to Register RHEL 5.2 against SMT

1. Install the suseRegisterRES package.

```
yum install suseRegisterRES
```

 Note: Additional Packages

You may need to install the `perl-Crypt-SSLeay` and `perl-XML-Parser` packages from the original RHEL media.

2. Copy the SMT certificate to the system:

```
wget http://smt-server.domain.top/smt.crt
```

```
cat smt.crt >> /etc/pki/tls/cert.pem
```

3. Edit `/etc/suseRegister.conf` to point to SMT by changing the URL value to

```
url: https://smt-server.domain.top/center/regsvc/
```

or (for SUSE Customer Center)

```
url = https://smt-server.domain.top/connect/
```

4. Register the system:

```
suse_register
```

8.9.5   How to Register RHEL 4.7 and RHEL 3.9 against SMT

1. Install the `suseRegisterRES` package:

```
up2date --get suseRegisterRES
up2date --get perl-XML-Writer
rpm -ivh /var/spool/up2date/suseRegisterRES*.rpm /var/spool/up2date/perl-XML-
Writer-0*.rpm
```

 Note: Additional Packages

You may need to install the `perl-Crypt-SSLeay` and `perl-XML-Parser` packages from the original RHEL media.

2. Copy the SMT certificate to the system:

```
wget http://smt-server.domain.top/smt.crt
```

```
cat smt.crt >> /usr/share/ssl/cert.pem
```

3. Edit `/etc/suseRegister.conf` to point to SMT by changing the URL value to

```
url = https://smt-server.domain.top/center/regsvc/
```

or (for SUSE Customer Center)

```
url = https://smt-server.domain.top/connect/
```

4. Register the system:

```
suse_register
```

A SMT REST API

The SMT REST interface is meant for communication with SMT clients and integration into other WebServices. The base URI for all the following REST calls is `https://YOURSMTSERV-ER/=/1`. The SMT server responds with XML data described for each call by an RNC snippet with comments.

Quick Reference

 Note: API for authenticating SMT clients.
Used internally in the `smt-client` package. Not intended for general administrative use!

GET /jobs	get list of all jobs for client
GET /job/@next	get the next job for client
GET /job/<jobid>	get job with jobid for client.
	Note: this marks the job as retrieved
PUT /job/<jobid>	update job having <jobid> using XML data.
	Note: updates only retrieved jobs

For backward compatibility reasons, the following are also available:

GET /jobs/@next	same as GET /job/@next
GET /jobs/<jobid>	same as GET /job/<jobid>
PUT /jobs/<jobid>	same as PUT /job/<jobid>

API for general access (this needs authentication using credentials from the `[REST]` section of `smt.conf`).

GET /client	get data of all clients
GET /client/<GUID>	get data of client with specified GUID
GET /client/<GUID>/jobs	get client's job data
GET /client/<GUID>/patchstatus	get client's patch status
GET /client/<GUID>/job/@next	get client's next job
GET /client/<GUID>/job/<jobid>	get specified client job data
GET /client/@all/jobs	get job data of all clients

```
GET /client/@all/patchstatus        get patch status of all clients
GET /repo                           get all repositories known to SMT
GET /repo/<repoid>                  get details of repository with <repoid>
GET /repo/<repoid>/patches          get repository's patches
GET /patch/<patchid>                get patch <patchid> details
GET /product                        get list of all products known to SMT
GET /product/<productid>            get details of product with <productid>
GET /product/<productid>/repos      get list of product's repositories
```

For backward compatibility reasons, plural forms are also available; e.g.:

```
GET /clients                        same as GET /client
GET /repos                          same as GET /repo
GET /product                        same as GET /product
```

Detailed Description

API for authenticating clients:

GET /jobs

Get list of all jobs for an authenticating client. When getting the jobs via this path they will not be set to the status retrieved.

Example:

```
<jobs>
  <job name="Patchstatus Job" created="2010-06-18 16:34:38"
  description="Patchstatus Job for Client 456" exitcode="" expires=""
  finished="" guid="456" guid_id="30" id="31" message="" parent_id=""
  persistent="1" retrieved="" status="0" stderr="" stdout="" targeted=""
  timelag="23:00:00" type="1" verbose="0">
    <arguments></arguments>
  </job>
  <job name="Software Push" created="2010-06-18 16:37:59"
  description="Software Push: mmv, whois" exitcode="" expires=""
  finished="" guid="456" guid_id="30" id="32" message="" parent_id=""
  persistent="0" retrieved="" status="0" stderr="" stdout="" targeted=""
  timelag="" type="2" verbose="0">
    <arguments>
      <packages>
```

```xml
      <package>mmv</package>
      <package>whois</package>
    </packages>
  </arguments>
 </job>
 <job name="Update Job" created="2010-06-18 16:38:39" description="Update
Job" exitcode="" expires="" finished="" guid="456" guid_id="30" id="34"
message="" parent_id="" persistent="0" retrieved="" status="0" stderr=""
stdout="" targeted="" timelag="" type="3" verbose="0">
 </job>
 <job name="Execute" created="2010-06-18 17:40:10" description="Execute
custom command" exitcode="0" expires="" finished="2010-06-18 17:40:14"
guid="456" guid_id="30" id="41" message="execute successfully finished"
parent_id="" persistent="0" retrieved="2010-06-18 17:40:14" status="1"
stderr="man:x:13:62:Manual pages viewer:/var/cache/man:/bin/bash"
stdout="" targeted="" timelag="" type="4" verbose="1">
  <arguments command="grep man /etc/passwd" />
 </job>
 <job name="Reboot" created="2010-06-18 16:40:28" description="Reboot
now" exitcode="" expires="2011-06-12 15:15:15" finished="" guid="456"
guid_id="30" id="37" message="" parent_id="" persistent="0" retrieved=""
status="0" stderr="" stdout="" targeted="2010-06-12 15:15:15" timelag=""
type="5" verbose="0">
 </job>
 <job name="Wait 5 sec. for exit 0." created="2010-06-18 16:40:59"
description="Wait for 5 seconds and return with value 0." exitcode=""
expires="" finished="" guid="456" guid_id="30" id="38" message=""
parent_id="" persistent="0" retrieved="" status="0" stderr="" stdout=""
targeted="" timelag="" type="7" verbose="0">
   <arguments exitcode="0" waittime="5" />
 </job>
 <job name="Eject job" created="2010-06-18 16:42:00" description="Job to
eject the CD/DVD drawer" exitcode="" expires="" finished="" guid="456"
guid_id="30" id="39" message="" parent_id="" persistent="0" retrieved=""
```

```
 status="0" stderr="" stdout="" targeted="" timelag="" type="8"
 verbose="0">
    <arguments action="toggle" />
  </job>
</jobs>
```

GET /jobs/@next

Get the next job for an authenticating client. The job will not be set to the retrieved status.

Example:

```
<job id="31" guid="456" type="patchstatus" verbose="false">
  <arguments></arguments>
</job>
```

GET /jobs/<jobid>

Get a job with the specified jobid for an authenticating client. The job will be set to the retrieved status.

When the client retrieves a job, not all the metadata is part of the XML response. However, it can be the full set of metadata, as **smt-client** only picks the data that is relevant. But a job retrieval should only contain the minimal set of data that is required to fulfill it.

RNC:

```
start = element job {
  attribute id {xsd:integer},        # the job ID. A job id alone is not
  unique.

                                     # A job is only uniquely identified
  with

                                     # guid and id. The same jobs for
  multiple

                                     # clients have the same job id.
  attribute parent_id {xsd:integer}?, # ID of the job on which this job
  depends
  attribute guid {xsd:string},
  attribute guid_id {xsd:integer}?,   # internal database ID of the client
```

```
                                          # (for compatibility reasons, if
third
                                          # party application talks to SMT
REST
                                          # service).
 attribute type {                         # job type ID string. Must be unique
and
                                          # equal to the name of the Perl
module on
                                          # the client.
   "softwarepush",
   "patchstatus",
   "<custom>"                             # add your own job types
 },
 attribute name {xsd:string},            # short custom name of the job,
user-defined
 attribute description {xsd:string},     # custom description of what the job
does
 attribute created {xsd:string},         # time stamp of creation
 attribute expires {xsd:string},         # expiration time stamp; the job
expires
                                          # if not retrieved by then
 attribute finished {xsd:string},        # time stamp of job completion
 attribute retrieved {xsd:string},       # time stamp of retrieval of the job
 attribute persistent {xsd:boolean}?,    # defines whether the job is a
persistent
                                          # (repetitive) job
 attribute verbose {xsd:boolean},        # if true, output of job commands is
                                          # attached to the result
 attribute exitcode {xsd:integer},       # the last exit code of the system
command
                                          # executed to complete the job
 attribute message {xsd:string},         # custom human-readable message the
client
                                          # sends back as a result
 attribute status {                      # logical status of the job
```

```
    0,        # not yet worked on: The job may be already retrieved but no
              # result was sent back yet.
    1,        # success: The job was retrieved, processed and the client sent
              # back a success response.
    2,        # failed: The job was retrieved, processed and the client sent
              # back a failure response.
    3},       # denied by client: The job was retrieved but could not be
              # processed as the client denied to process this job type
              # (a client needs to allow all job types that should be
processed,
              # any other will be denied).
  attribute stderr {text},        # standard error output of jobs's
system
                                  # commands (filled if verbose)
  attribute stdout {text},        # standard output of jobs's system
                                  # commands (filled if verbose)
  attribute targeted {xsd:string},   # time stamp when this job will be
                                  # delivered at the earliest
  attribute timelag {xsd:string}?,   # interval time of a persistent job
  in
                                  # the format "HH:MM:SS" (HH can be
                                  # bigger than 23)
  element-arguments               # job-type-specific XML data
}
```

Example (minimal job definition for a 'softwarepush' job):

```
<job id="32" guid="456" type="softwarepush" verbose="false">
  <arguments>
    <packages>
      <package>mmv</package>
      <package>whois</package>
    </packages>
  </arguments>
</job>
```

```
PUT /job/<jobid>
```

Update a job for an authenticating client using XML data.

A client can only send job results for jobs properly retrieved previously. The jobs will be set to status done (with the exception of persistent jobs, in which case a new target time will be computed).

Examples:

- Example for a successful patchstatus job:

```
<job id="31" guid="abc123" exitcode="0" message="0:0:0:0 #
PackageManager=0 Security=0 Recommended=0 Optional=0" status="1"
stderr="" stdout="" />
```

- Example for a failed softwarepush:

```
<job id="32" guid="abc123" exitcode="104" message="softwarepush
failed" status="2" stderr="" stdout="" />
```

- Example for a successful update:

```
<job id="34" guid="abc123" exitcode="0" message="update successfully
finished" status="1" stderr="" stdout="" />
```

- Example for a successful reboot job:

```
<job id="37" guid="abc123" exitcode="0" message="reboot triggered"
status="1" stderr="" stdout="" />
```

- Execute for a successful wait job:

```
<job id="38" guid="abc123" exitcode="0" message="wait successfully
finished" status="1" stderr="" stdout="" />
```

- Example for a successful eject job:

```
<job id="39" guid="abc123" exitcode="0" message="eject successfully
finished" status="1" stderr="" stdout="" />
```

- Example for a successful execute job:

```
<job id="41" guid="abc123" exitcode="0" message="execute successfully
  finished" status="1" stderr="man:x:13:62:Manual pages viewer:/var/
cache/man:/bin/bash" stdout="" />
```

API for general access:

GET /repo/<repoid>

Returns detailed information about the specified repository. The <repoid> can be obtained using the /repos or /products/<productid>/repos/ call.

RNC:

```
start = element repo {                        # repository
  attribute id {xsd:integer},                 # SMT ID of the repository
  attribute name {xsd:string},                # repository's Unix name
  attribute target {xsd:string},              # repository's target product
  attribute type {"nu" | "yum" | "zypp" | "pum"}, # type of repository
  element description {xsd:string},           # description of the repository
  element localpath {xsd:string},             # path to local SMT mirror of
the
                                              # repository
  element url {xsd:anyURI},                   # original URL of the
repository
  element mirrored {
    attribute date {xsd:integer}              # timestamp of the last
successful
                                              # mirror (empty if not mirrored
yet)
  }
}
```

Example:

```
<repo name="SLES10-SP2-Updates" id="226" target="sles-10-i586" type="nu">
  <description>SLES10-SP2-Updates for sles-10-i586</description>
  <localpath>/local/htdocs/repo/$RCE/SLES10-SP2-Updates/sles-10-i586</
localpath>
  <mirrored date="1283523440"/>
```

```
    <url>https://nu.novell.com/repo/$RCE/SLES10-SP2-Updates/sles-10-i586/</
url>
  </repo>
```

GET /repo/<repoid>/patches

Returns a list of all patches in the specified software repository. The repoid can be
obtained using the /repos or /products/<productid>/repos/ call.
RNC:

```
start = element patches {
  element patch {
    attribute id {xsd:integer},        # SMT ID of the patch
    attribute name {xsd:string},       # patch's Unix name
    attribute version {xsd:integer}    # patch's version number
    attribute category {              # patch importance category
      "security",
      "recommended",
      "optional",
      "mandatory"}
  }*
}
```

Example:

```
<patches>
  <patch name="slesp2-krb5" category="security" id="1471" version="6775"/>
  <patch name="slesp2-heartbeat" category="recommended" id="1524"
 version="5857"/>
  <patch name="slesp2-curl" category="security" id="1409" version="6402"/>
  ...
</patches>
```

GET /repos

Returns a list of all software repositories known to SMT. Those which are currently
mirrored on SMT have non-empty mirror time stamp in the mirrored attribute.
RNC:

```
start = element repos {
```

SMT REST API

```
  element repo {
    attribute id {xsd:integer},         # SMT ID of the repository
    attribute name {xsd:string},        # repository's Unix name
    attribute target {xsd:string},      # repository's target product
    attribute mirrored {xsd:integer}    # time stamp of the last successful
 mirror

                                        # (empty if not mirrored yet)

  }*
}
```

Example:

```
<repos>
  <repo name="SLE10-SDK-Updates" id="1" mirrored="" target="sles-10-
x86_64"/>
  <repo name="SLE10-SDK-SP3-Pool" id="2" mirrored="" target="sles-10-ppc"/
>
  <repo name="SLES10-SP2-Updates" id="226" mirrored="1283523440"
 target="sles-10-i586"/>
  ...
</repo>
```

GET /patch/<patchid>

Returns detailed information about the specified patch. The patchid can be obtained via the /repo/<repoid>/patches call.

RNC:

```
start = element patch {
  attribute id {xsd:integer},           # SMT ID of the patch
  attribute name {xsd:string},          # patch's Unix name
  attribute version {xsd:integer},      # patch's version number
  attribute category {                  # patch importance category
    "security",
    "recommended",
    "optional",
    "mandatory"},
  element title {xsd:string},           # title of the patch
```

```
  element description {text},              # description of issues fixed by
the patch
  element issued {
    attribute date {xsd:integer}           # patch release time stamp
  },
  element packages {                       # packages which need update as
part
                                           # of this patch
    element package {                      # individual RPM package data
      attribute name {xsd:string},         # package name
      attribute epoch {xsd:integer},       # epoch number
      attribute version {xsd:string},      # version string
      attribute release {xsd:string},      # release string
      attribute arch {xsd:string},         # architecture string
      element origlocation {xsd:anyURI},   # URL of the RPM package in the
                                           # original repository
      element smtlocation {xsd:anyURI}     # URL of the RPM package at the
SMT server
    }*
  },
  element references {                     # references to issues fixed by
this
                                           # patch
    element reference {                    # individual reference details
      attribute id,                        # ID number of the issue
(bugzilla
                                           # or CVE number)
      attribute title {xsd:string},        # issue title
      attribute type {"bugzilla","cve"},   # type of the issue
      attribute href {xsd:anyURI}          # URL of the issue in its issue
                                           # tracking system
    }*
  }
}
```

Example:

```
<patch name="slesp2-krb5" category="security" id="1471" version="6775">
  <description>
    Specially crafted AES and RC4 packets could allow unauthenticated
    remote attackers to trigger an integer overflow leads to heap memory
    corruption (CVE-2009-4212). This has been fixed.
    Specially crafted AES and RC4 packets could allow
    unauthenticated remote attackers to trigger an integer
    overflow leads to heap memory corruption (CVE-2009-4212).
  </description>
  <issued date="1263343020"/>
  <packages>
    <package name="krb5" arch="i586" epoch="" release="19.43.2"
version="1.4.3">
      <origlocation>https://nu.novell.com/repo/$RCE/SLES10-SP2-Updates/
sles-10-i586/rpm/i586/krb5-1.4.3-19.43.2.i586.rpm</origlocation>
      <smtlocation>http://kompost.suse.cz/repo/$RCE/SLES10-SP2-Updates/
sles-10-i586/rpm/i586/krb5-1.4.3-19.43.2.i586.rpm</smtlocation>
    </package>
    <package name="krb5-apps-servers" arch="i586" epoch=""
 release="19.43.2" version="1.4.3">
      <origlocation>https://nu.novell.com/repo/$RCE/SLES10-SP2-Updates/
sles-10-i586/rpm/i586/krb5-apps-servers-1.4.3-19.43.2.i586.rpm</
origlocation>
      <smtlocation>http://kompost.suse.cz/repo/$RCE/SLES10-SP2-Updates/
sles-10-i586/rpm/i586/krb5-apps-servers-1.4.3-19.43.2.i586.rpm</
smtlocation>
    </package>
    ...
  </packages>
  <references>
    <reference id="535943" href="https://bugzilla.suse.com/show_bug.cgi?
id=535943" title="bug number 535943" type="bugzilla"/>
    <reference id="CVE-2009-4212" href="http://cve.mitre.org/cgi-bin/
cvename.cgi?name=CVE-2009-4212" title="CVE-2009-4212" type="cve"/>
```

```
    </references>
    <title>Security update for Kerberos 5</title>
  </patch>
```

GET /products

Returns list of all products known to SMT.

RNC:

```
start element products {
  element product {
    attribute id {xsd:integer},      # SMT ID of the product
    attribute name {xsd:string},     # Unix name of the product
    attribute version {xsd:string},  # version string
    attribute rel {xsd:string},      # release string
    attribute arch {xsd:string},     # target machine architecture string
    attribute uiname {xsd:string}    # name of the product to be
                                     # displayed to users
  }*
}
```

Example:

```
<products>
  <product name="SUSE_SLED" arch="x86_64" id="1824" rel="" uiname="SUSE
Linux Enterprise Desktop 11 SP1" version="11.1"/>
  <product name="SUSE_SLES" arch="i686" id="1825" rel="" uiname="SUSE
Linux Enterprise Server 11 SP1" version="11.1"/>
  <product name="sle-hae" arch="i686" id="1880" rel="" uiname="SUSE Linux
Enterprise High Availability Extension 11 SP1" version="11.1"/>
  <product name="SUSE-Linux-Enterprise-Thin-Client" arch="" id="940"
rel="SP1" uiname="SUSE Linux Enterprise 10 Thin Client SP1" version="10"/
>
  ...
</products>
```

```
GET /product/<productid>
```

Returns information about the specified product. The productid can be obtained from data returned by the /products call.

RNC:

```
start = element product {
  attribute id {xsd:integer},        # SMT ID of the product
  attribute name {xsd:string},       # Unix name of the product
  attribute version {xsd:string},    # version string
  attribute rel {xsd:string},        # release string
  attribute arch {xsd:string},       # target machine architecture string
  attribute uiname {xsd:string}      # name of the product to be displayed
                                     # to users
}
```

Example:

```
<product name="SUSE_SLED" arch="x86_64" id="1824" rel="" uiname="SUSE
 Linux Enterprise Server 11 SP1" version="11.1"/>
```

```
GET /product/<productid>/repos
```

Returns the list of all software repositories for the specified product. The productid can be obtained from the data returned by the /products call.

RNC:

See the /repos call.

Example:

```
<repos>
  <repo name="SLED11-SP1-Updates" id="143" mirrored="" target="sle-11-
x86_64"/>
  <repo name="SLE11-SP1-Debuginfo-Pool" id="400" mirrored=""
 target="sle-11-x86_64"/>
  <repo name="SLED11-Extras" id="417" mirrored="" target="sle-11-x86_64"/>
  <repo name="SLED11-SP1-Pool" id="215" mirrored="" target="sle-11-
x86_64"/>
  <repo name="nVidia-Driver-SLE11-SP1" id="469" mirrored="" target=""/>
  <repo name="ATI-Driver-SLE11-SP1" id="411" mirrored="" target=""/>
```

```
  <repo name="SLE11-SP1-Debuginfo-Updates" id="6" mirrored=""
 target="sle-11-x86_64"/>
</repos>
```

B Documentation Updates

This chapter lists content changes for this document.

This manual was updated on the following dates:

- Section B.1, "December 2015 (Initial Release of SUSE Linux Enterprise Desktop 12 SP1)"

B.1 December 2015 (Initial Release of SUSE Linux Enterprise Desktop 12 SP1)

General

- *SMT Guide* is now part of the documentation for SUSE Linux Enterprise Desktop.

- Add-ons provided by SUSE have been renamed to modules and extensions. The manuals have been updated to reflect this change.

- Numerous small fixes and additions to the documentation, based on technical feedback.

- The registration service has been changed from Novell Customer Center to SUSE Customer Center.

- In YaST, you will now reach *Network Settings* via the *System* group. *Network Devices* is gone (https://bugzilla.suse.com/show_bug.cgi?id=867809).

Chapter 1, SMT Installation

- Rewrote and simplified the whole installation procedure as SMT is now part of SUSE Linux Enterprise Server.

- Updated *Section 1.2, "Upgrading from Previous Versions of SMT"* to describe ways to upgrade to version 12 SP1, including migration to SUSE Customer Center.

- Updated suseRegister to SUSEConnect and introduced new `namespace` option in *Section 3.5, "Using the Test Environment"* **and** *Section 3.6, "Testing and Filtering Update Repositories with Staging".*

- Removed SUSE Linux Enterprise Server 9 references and informed about dropped support.

Chapter 7, SMT Tools and Configuration Files

- Added `jobStatusIsSuccess`, `mirror_preunlock_hook`, and `mirror_postunlock_hook` options in *Section 7.2.1, "/etc/smt.conf".*

- Added **smt-setup-custom-catalogs** as an alias for **smt-setup-custom-repos** in *Section 7.1.2, "/usr/sbin/smt Commands".*

- Removed the redundant **smt-scc-sync** command description from *Section 7.1.2, "/usr/sbin/smt Commands".*

- Removed SUSE Linux Enterprise Server 9 references and fixed command names and a log file name.

Chapter 8, Configuring Clients to Use SMT

- Updated the way the client accepts untrusted certificate from SMT in the introduction to *Chapter 8, Configuring Clients to Use SMT.*

- Added *Section 8.8, "Online Migration of SUSE Linux Enterprise Clients".*

- Added SUSE Linux Enterprise 12 support to *Section 8.3, "Configuring Clients with the clientSetup4SMT.sh Script in SLE 11 and 12".*

- Added *Section 8.2.2, "Configuring SUSE Linux Enterprise 12 Clients".*

- Added *Section 8.6, "Registering SLE12 Clients against SMT Test Environment".*

Bugfixes

- Rephrased the paragraph and updated contact e-mails in *Tip: Merging Multiple Organization Site Credentials* (https://bugzilla.suse.com/show_bug.cgi?id=866936).